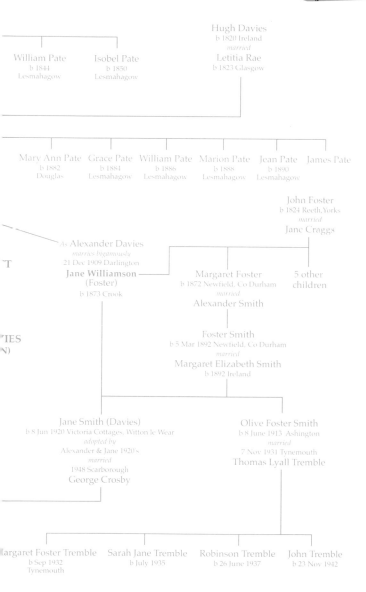

Hugh Davies
b 1820 Ireland
married
Letitia Rae
b 1823 Glasgow

William Pate
b 1844
Lesmahagow

Isobel Pate
b 1850
Lesmahagow

Mary Ann Pate
b 1882
Douglas

Grace Pate
b 1884
Lesmahagow

William Pate
b 1886
Lesmahagow

Marion Pate
b 1888
Lesmahagow

Jean Pate
b 1890
Lesmahagow

James Pate

John Foster
b 1824 Reeth, Yorks
married
Jane Craggs

As Alexander Davies
marries bigamously
21 Dec 1909 Darlington
Jane Williamson
(Foster)
b 1873 Crook

T

Margaret Foster
b 1872 Newfield, Co Durham
married
Alexander Smith

5 other
children

Foster Smith
b 5 Mar 1892 Newfield, Co Durham
married
Margaret Elizabeth Smith
b 1892 Ireland

IES
N)

Jane Smith (Davies)
b 8 Jun 1920 Victoria Cottages, Witton le Wear
adopted by
Alexander & Jane 1920's
married
1948 Scarborough
George Crosby

Olive Foster Smith
b 8 June 1913 Ashington
married
7 Nov 1931 Tynemouth
Thomas Lyall Tremble

Margaret Foster Tremble
b Sep 1932
Tynemouth

Sarah Jane Tremble
b July 1935

Robinson Tremble
b 26 June 1937

John Tremble
b 23 Nov 1942

The Real Story of Finding her Father

SEEKING CATHERINE COOKSON'S 'DA'

The Real Story of Finding her Father

SEEKING CATHERINE COOKSON'S 'DA'

Kathleen Jones

CONSTABLE • LONDON

Constable & Robinson Ltd
3 The Lanchesters
162 Fulham Palace Road
London W6 9ER
www.constablerobinson.com

First published in the UK by Constable,
an imprint of Constable & Robinson Ltd 2004

A copy of the British Library Cataloguing in
Publication Data is available from the British Library

ISBN 1-84119-845-5

Printed and bound in the EU

CONTENTS

ILLUSTRATIONS

INTRODUCTION

Catherine Cookson was one of the most successful authors of all time. Born into considerable poverty in the north-east of England in 1906, the illegitimate daughter of a barmaid, Catherine received little formal education, but still went on to write over a hundred books – almost all of them bestsellers; she was made a Dame of the British Empire and became one of the most highly paid authors in the world. Her phenomenal success has generated endless fascination. Catherine herself admitted that she was driven to keep on writing by bleak internal forces, and that her determination to succeed and become 'somebody' was rooted in childhood rejection and the shame of her illegitimate birth.

The fame and fortune she set out to win was a long time in coming. Although she had been writing stories since she was a child, her first novel wasn't published until she was forty-three. For a long time she tried to escape her roots – of which she was deeply ashamed – and write the kind of ladylike novels she found on the library shelves. Her first efforts were disappointing, mainly because her stories lacked the illusion of reality that readers were looking for. Catherine simply didn't know enough about the people whose lives she was trying to describe; she didn't understand their concerns or their motivations. Desperate to get published, she joined a local writers' group, and once a week in the public library subjected her work to collective criticism. The results weren't encouraging. She even sent a play she had written to an agency that promised a professional reader's report. It came back with these words scribbled on the back page: 'Strongly advise author to give up writing'. This comment would have daunted most people, but not Catherine. She was even more determined to be published.

The pivotal moment of Catherine Cookson's career as a writer came in 1947, one wet, windy night in Hastings. Members of the writers' circle, bracing themselves for yet another awkward saga of the rich, landed gentry whose lives Catherine could only hazily imagine, never forgot how the forty-one-year-old author read a powerful, moving story called 'The Girl who had no Da'. It was her own story, an account of the moment when, taunted by children in the street, she discovered that she was illegitimate, the child of an unknown man who had deserted her mother before she was born. Catherine had never before written with the intensity of painful personal experience and she was so afraid of her audience's response that she had to read the story sitting down because her legs were shaking so much. But its impact was immediate and Catherine remembered long afterwards how the group stood up and clapped and clapped. She left the library that evening knowing that this should be the real material for her stories, the rich seam of childhood experience that she would mine again and again for over a hundred books. It was the golden lode that made her one of the best-selling novelists of all time and one of the richest women in the world.

Fifty-two years after that momentous night in Hastings, on a cold November afternoon in 1998, I attended Catherine Cookson's memorial service in Newcastle's Roman Catholic Cathedral. The church was already packed and there were still people outside waiting to come in. Everyone in the north-east seemed to want to bid a final farewell. In the days and weeks after Catherine's death there had been numerous tributes in newspapers, magazines and on television and radio. As her biographer I had studied them all. Catherine's voice came over clear and certain, talking about her life, her childhood, and in particular the fact that she was illegitimate. It was increasingly apparent to me, as I researched her life, that her unknown father's absence and his rejection of both Catherine and her mother Kate went to the root of her character and was at the heart of everything she did. She returned to it in every interview she gave. 'I wanted to make something of myself,' she said repeatedly. 'I was going to show them.' It was the driving motivation that took her away from the north-east to live in the south, and the mainspring of her imagination.

The mystery of her father's identity became an obsession. Catherine spent her whole life imagining and inventing him for herself. As a young child, her favourite means of escape from the difficult circumstances in which she lived was a fantasy that her father was a rich aristocrat and that one day he would come to look for her and take her away to live in the luxury of his stately home. It was tragic that, in a life that spanned over ninety years, Catherine was never able to get over the fact of her illegitimacy. The social stigma was one she shared with a great many other people in public life, as well as on the streets of Jarrow – there were a lot of 'baskets', as her mother Kate euphemistically called them. Perhaps it was the feeling that her unknown father had abandoned her because he considered her worthless that had cut to the bone. As I sat in the pew at the memorial service and listened to the tributes and to Catherine's recorded voice talking about her life, I wondered who her father had been – and whether there was anyone in that church, among Catherine's extended family, who actually knew. It was the last great mystery of her life – and one I decided to try to solve. I began with the story that Catherine herself told about her mother's love affair with a mysterious, handsome stranger.

1

OUR KATE

On a cool afternoon in 1904, a tall, slim man walked into the saloon bar of the Ravensworth Arms in the village of Lamesley in County Durham. He was beautifully dressed, in contrast to the mine-workers who packed the public bar on pay days, and spoke with an attractive lilt to his voice. The bar staff noted his sleek black top hat, the black overcoat with an astrakhan collar and the silver-topped cane in his gloved hands. These were the accoutrements of a gentleman and he had the manners to match. His name, he said, was Alexander Davies and he was in the area on business – though what that business was he didn't disclose. At twenty-six he was charming, with the kind of good looks that attracted women without any effort on his part. One of his daughters later described him as being the spitting image of that early star of silent films, Rudolph Valentino.

Behind the bar was twenty-two-year-old Kate Fawcett, intelligent, pretty and sociable. Kate had come to the pub after being 'in service' at nearby Ravensworth Castle. While working there she had struck up a friendship with Jenny, the pub owner's daughter, and she and her younger sister Mary both came to work at the Ravensworth Arms, Kate as a barmaid and occasional cook, Mary as a chambermaid. The girls lived in, sleeping in one of the rooms in the attic. It was easier and more congenial work than the drudgery of a parlourmaid at the Castle and Kate was much happier there.

Kate and her sister Mary had had a difficult life. Their mother Rose McConnell was one of a large family of Irish immigrants living just outside Jarrow, south of the Tyne, and scraping a living from a smallholding called Grange Farm. When Rose married William Fawcett, a worker at the steel mills, they lived with her parents in a cramped house with fourteen other people. It wasn't until Rose was

Reconstruction of the kitchen at No. 10, New Buildings, Jarrow.

expecting her third child Sarah that they moved into bigger lodgings in Jarrow. There, Sarah, Kate and their younger sister Mary were born. And it was there that William died from tuberculosis, the scourge of large industrial cities in the nineteenth century. Rose moved back into her parents' house with her five daughters and went out to work in the iron puddling mills to support them. Her two eldest daughters died of TB shortly afterwards. Soon, however, Rose met another Irish immigrant – John McMullen, a dock-worker, one of triplets who had recently been discharged from the Indian Army and come over to the Tyne to look for work. She married him and shortly afterwards had another child – a son they called John, after his father, though he was always known as Jack.

Kate remembered the crushing poverty. The docks were no longer a regular source of work, in a decline that had begun in the second half of the nineteenth century. For the workforce, the problem was that there were no permanent jobs. Dockers were taken on by the day and sometimes by the hour. When a ship came in and needed to be offloaded or loaded with a new cargo, the necessary labour would be taken on. Those wanting work used to go every day to the dock gates where the foremen would choose who they were going to employ. They could then discriminate against those they considered troublemakers, or men they thought weren't physically fit enough to work quickly. There was rarely enough work to employ all those who stood expectantly outside the gates, and many were sent home with no prospect of employment or money in their pockets to feed their family.

John McMullen fared better than most because he was a good worker, but even he couldn't expect full employment – the cargoes simply weren't there. When the dock gates were shut in his face and his pockets were empty, Kate and one of her sisters would be sent barefoot around the streets in better-off areas to beg. Kate was chosen because she had a limp – the result of one foot being slightly twisted in the womb, which had never been put right. On one occasion – in the middle of winter – a woman felt so sorry for Kate she gave her a pair of boots but when she got home Rose took them off her and pawned them for the money. Much of the money went on drink. It was the anaesthetic of the poor and both Rose and John liked a tipple. Unfortunately when John drank he became violent, smashing household furniture, fighting, singing and hitting his wife and stepdaughters freely if they tried to interfere. Even when sober he was a strict stepfather, taking the belt to the girls when they stepped out of line. On one occasion, when twenty-year-old Sarah went up to Newcastle to visit a relative, she missed the last tram back and had to stay the night. Her stepfather didn't believe her story and she was belted black and blue when she arrived home.

When Kate was twelve she was sent out to service with a butcher's family, helping with the housework and doing the laundry, even though she was so small she had to stand on a stool to stir the boiling sheets and aprons in the set pot. She worked long days – from six-thirty in the morning until late in the evening, with only one half day off per fortnight – all for two shillings and sixpence a week (about twelve pence at today's reckoning). Her sisters too, when they reached the age

The Jarrow tram outside the entrance to Tyne Dock.

of twelve, had to go out to work. Kate eventually graduated to the position of nursemaid to a rich family and with them she experienced her first trips away from Newcastle and got a glimpse of a better life – a world that girls like Kate could only dream of. As nursemaid to the Pattersons, Kate even went on holiday to the Lake District – the first time she had ever been more than thirty miles from home. It was from this family that she earned her recommendation to Ravensworth Castle and life 'below stairs'. The Castle, owned by the Earls of Ravensworth, was one of the big stately homes of the north-east, occupying a commanding position on a hillside looking across the plains of county Durham towards the coast. It wasn't a genuine castle but a huge gothic extravaganza requiring armies of servants to keep it running. It was eventually pulled down when the family's fortunes changed for the worse in the 1930s and woodland now covers the site.

Kate was 'in service' at the Castle just after the death of Queen Victoria, in the heady days of Edwardian frivolity at the beginning of Edward VII's reign. Victorian respectability gave way to the indulgence of pleasure and a rather more decadent atmosphere. How much of this change of attitude penetrated the servants' hall is difficult to know. Homes such as Ravensworth Castle were still run on almost feudal lines, with everyone knowing their place and keeping it. Kate was a popular girl with other members of the staff and at the Christmas Ball danced with the butler. She was then, apparently, singled out to dance with one of the guests – something that soon had tongues wagging. But high-class servitude didn't suit Kate. She had already met Jenny, whose parents owned the Ravensworth Arms, and when they offered her a job, she left the Castle.

Lamesley is a strange little village, a collection of farms and houses strung out along several country lanes, without an obvious centre. A church and a farm stand at the crossroads and about a quarter of a mile down the road to Tanfield is the Ravensworth Arms. It's a big, sprawling building that has been altered and added to over the centuries since its beginning as a small coaching inn. In Kate's time it was the main watering hole in the village, serving people from the Castle whose gates were only a short walk away, as well as the farmers and miners living in the vicinity. The public bar could be a little rough, but the saloon bar had a very different clientele.

Behind the bar Kate was used to being chatted up by hopeful pit lads and customers and she was practised at fending off their advances. She still dreamed of better things. In her imagination she would meet someone who would take her away from the grinding poverty she had been brought up with. She told her sisters that she was not going to marry a miner, or a docker. So when the well-dressed and apparently respectable Alexander Davies deployed his charm across the saloon bar on that fateful afternoon, Kate was vulnerable.

The Ravensworth Arms.

*Mineworkers,
including men and boys.*

Attractive, warm-hearted and 'wanting love', in her daughter's words, she responded to his advances and began 'walking out' with him whenever his business interests brought him to Lamesley. Alexander was similarly smitten; according to eyewitnesses he was 'head over heels' the moment he saw Kate.

Her sister Mary was not quite so impressed. Alec, as they soon called him, was a gentleman and what would a real gentleman want with Kate? Catherine later said that Mary had only said it to 'hurt Kate' and make her daughter more ashamed of her. When Catherine questioned her aunt closely, the evidence of Alexander's genteel birth was based purely on his appearance and his beautiful voice. Catherine blamed Mary for misleading her because, in stating his identity as a gentleman so emphatically, Mary had created for her niece 'a sense of false superiority and a burning desire to meet this wonderful creature'.* In middle age, after Catherine had had the opportunity to talk to her mother about him, she said that she always put the word 'gentleman' in inverted commas. The inference was that, although Mary had been taken in by appearances like everyone else, Alexander wasn't genuine. At the time, although deeply in love, even Kate felt the need to be cautious. She later told Catherine that she had suspected right from the beginning that he wasn't free and that his extravagant promises were false. He was vague about where he was living, vague about his business interests, and there were long, unexplained absences. But after two years of this on–off courtship, Alexander's persuasiveness became too

*From the Catherine Cookson Collection in the Howard Gotlieb Archival Research Centre at Boston University.

difficult to resist. Possibly weakened by the drink she liked but had no head for, Kate's resolve faltered and she allowed him to make love to her. He promised that he was going to marry her and she considered herself engaged.

This episode was followed by one of Alexander's disappearing tricks. Like many women, Kate discovered that having allowed her lover to have what he had begged for, he vanished soon afterwards without explanation. This became even more distressing when she discovered that she was pregnant with his child. She was distraught. In those days, if their families wouldn't help, unmarried mothers were put in the workhouse to have their children. They were treated like criminals or delinquents, their children taken from them to be brought up in a separate section of the workhouse, and then they had to work – in the laundry, the kitchens or the wards – for fourteen years until the child was old enough to take a job in order to support him- or herself. This fourteen-year servitude was regarded as 'paying off their debt' to society for what was then considered to be a moral crime. Ending up in the workhouse was one of Kate's greatest fears. But if Alexander Davies didn't return to keep his promise and marry her, Kate had no confidence that John McMullen would do anything other than put her out of the door and into the workhouse. It was a terrible situation to be in.

When Catherine Cookson grew up and took a job in the laundry at Harton Workhouse, one of the things that distressed her most was having to escort the unmarried mothers – some of them little more than girls themselves – to the orphanage once a month to see their offspring. They always found it difficult to leave their children behind afterwards and

The grim façade of Harton Workhouse.

were often hysterical on the journey back. On one occasion, one of the girls was quite suicidal and threatened to throw herself off the coach. Their misery affected Catherine deeply. It gave her a greater insight into what her mother must have suffered when she discovered that she was pregnant.

By the time Kate was five months' gone and 'beginning to show' she had to leave the Ravensworth Arms in disgrace. Her lover had not returned, and in real fear Kate went back to Jarrow and confessed her condition to her mother and her stepfather. John McMullen took the belt to her, but he didn't put her out on the street. Instead a plan was devised, one adopted by many families in such a situation. The child would be brought up by John and Rose as their own, and Kate would go back to work to earn the money for its support. Grateful for their help, Kate endured the wagging tongues and the sneers every time she walked down the street, as well as the humiliation of knowing she had been abandoned by the man she'd trusted too well.

Then one day, when she was out with her mother, a man came to the door. He called himself Alec and asked for Kate. He said that he had gone to the Ravensworth Arms looking for her, and had been told that she had left and been given this address. When Kate returned and he saw her condition, he was apparently very concerned and behaved in a loving and responsible fashion. He invited Kate to spend the afternoon at the Newcastle races with him, was charming to Rose and generally created a good impression. Kate was ecstatic! On their day out he promised that they would be married very soon, and that he would find them somewhere to live and come back as soon as it was organized. Then, as he had done so often in the past, he vanished again.

Shortly afterwards Kate's child was born, in the only bedroom at 5 Leam Lane. It was a difficult labour – if Kate hadn't been punished already for her moral lapse, then she was certainly punished now. Her life was in danger and a doctor had to be summoned – no mean thing at a time when doctors were so expensive the poor could not afford to have them. But the doctor who attended the birth and eased Catherine into the world was someone who had chosen to work in that community because of his social conscience, and

Kate was one of the beneficiaries of his benevolence. She would be grateful for the rest of her life. As for Kate's daughter, the young Dr McHaffie became a fantasy father for the illegitimate girl as she grew older, and later featured as the hero of her first novel.

Catherine's novel *Kate Hannigan* opens with an account of the birth of Kate's illegitimate child in a poor tenement in Jarrow. It's a difficult confinement that tests all the young doctor's skill and Kate Hannigan almost dies. She feels utterly hopeless about her own prospects and those of her child. 'What chance has it?' she asks the doctor wearily. He tries to rally her spirits, but he's a newcomer to the area and Kate knows better than he does the prejudice and spite they will both have to live with. In the novel Catherine explores all the subtle rivalries and interdependencies of the 'fifteen streets' around Tyne Dock. Kate Hannigan's father – a recognizable portrait of John McMullen, sullen with anger – will not stir from the fireside even for his daughter. Kate's mother is too frightened of her husband to be of much use. Yet against any outside threat the Hannigans, like the McMullens, close ranks as a family.

All the grim realities of poverty are there in the opening pages of the novel. The drunken, venial midwife who is all that can be afforded. The fact that when the doctor calls for old sheets to be torn up to use for the birth he is laughed at for his ignorance – there are no sheets at all, new or old. The doctor is also laughed at for his humanity. The midwife condemns the way he treats Kate Hannigan as if she was the Duchess of Connaught, instead of a trollop going to bring a bastard into the world.

Leam Lane at the time of Catherine's birth.

Like her fictional counterpart the real Kate was fortunate. With the aid of chloroform – still something of an innovation – her daughter was dragged, struggling, into the world. After the birth, as soon as Kate was strong enough, Rose took her to Newcastle, to an address where they believed Alexander Davies was living. Kate told Catherine before she died that Alec had given her the address himself. It was a brave expedition, driven by extreme need. His absence couldn't be ignored any more – he must be told of his daughter's birth and be made to keep his promises. But when they reached the house the door was opened by a woman whose attitude was hostile. She denied that anyone called 'Alexander Davies' was living at that address. Catherine later used this episode in a novel called *Fenwick Houses*, where the character Christine – again based on her mother – sees a photograph on the piano that she recognizes as the man who has fathered her child, yet the woman at the door is able to deny his existence because he has altered his surname. In the book, the man has a double-barrelled name and only gives Christine part of it. This story, told to Catherine by her mother, would later form a crucial part of the jigsaw.

By the time she returned home, Kate was ill with worry and what was sometimes called 'milk fever'. She stubbornly refused to believe that this time Alexander really had abandoned her. He would come back and marry her, she insisted. The legal time limit for registration of a birth came and went. Kate still procrastinated. But then the fear of the legal penalties she might incur became too great. She went to the registrar in South Shields. To cover the delay she gave Catherine's date of birth as the 27 June rather than 20 June, and, unable to abandon the idea that Alexander might still come and make everything right, she told the registrar that she was married, describing herself as Catherine Davies, formerly Fawcett, and gave her husband's name as Alexander Davies, his occupation as 'Commission Agent'.

Later, ashamed of what she had done, Kate hid the birth certificate and never told anyone. Catherine Ann Fawcett, otherwise known as Catherine McMullen, didn't know until she was nearly thirty that she was actually called Catherine Ann Davies, or that she had a false date of birth in the official records. Afterwards Kate, grieving over her lover and wretched at having to leave her child, handed the baby to her

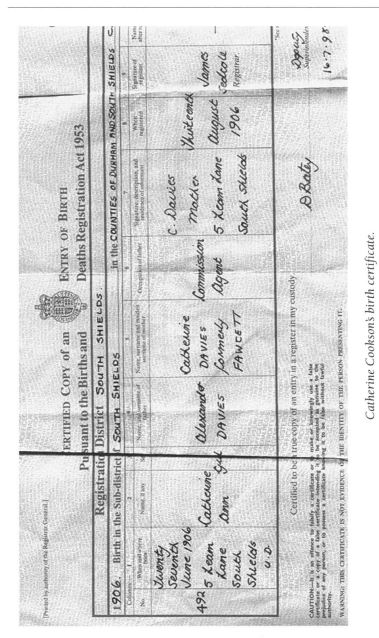

Catherine Cookson's birth certificate.

mother Rose and took a job with a baker in Gateshead. From then on she would only be able to see her child on her day off once a week. And she knew that she would never be able to tell Catherine that she was her mother; the family fiction would have to be preserved.

2

---∗---

THE GIRL WHO HAD NO DA

Catherine grew up, like many children in her situation, thinking that her grandparents – Rose and John McMullen – were her parents. She was known by everyone as Kitty or Katie McMullen. She regarded her uncle Jack and aunts Sarah and Mary as her brother and sisters. With Kate she had a special relationship. When Kate came to the house on her days off there would be little presents for Catherine and she would try to hug her and fuss over her – caresses which were shrugged off by the rather prickly little girl. And even if Catherine allowed herself to be cuddled by Kate, Rose would often snatch her away. Even as a small child Catherine sensed a tense atmosphere whenever Kate was there; the unspoken resentment between Rose and Kate, the money handed over, the curtailed affection. Children are very quick to detect atmospheres and it wasn't long before Catherine realized that Kate's position in the family was very different to that of her sisters Mary and Sarah.

When Catherine was about five years old, Rose and John moved from the two rooms in Leam Lane to a flat in what was called the 'New Buildings' in William Black Street. This

Photograph of the New Buildings Community in 1918.
Kate on the far right of the group, Catherine Centre.

was a larger flat, but there was still only a kitchen, a parlour and one bedroom to house three adults and a child. Rose and John slept in the small bedroom, with Catherine in a truckle bed which slid under the double bedstead during the day, and Jack – then a young man of about twenty – slept either on the settle in the kitchen or in a fold-down bed in the parlour. This was referred to as a 'dess-bed' (desk-bed) because during the day it folded up into a piece of furniture that looked like a bureau. This wasn't unusual – most working-class families coped with cramped accommodation in this way. Families were large and houses were small. My own Tyneside grandparents also had a 'dess-bed' in the living room for my uncle to sleep on.

The McMullens' move had been made without telling Kate, and when she arrived at the rooms in Leam Lane on her day off she was devastated to find that her family was no longer there. She imagined the worst – that they had been taken off to the workhouse, or done a moonlight flit for other reasons. Neighbours gave her the new address and she hurried up the hill to the New Buildings. Catherine remembered that day all her life: how she had seen Kate coming up the street very agitated, Kate's rough embrace, her anger towards Rose. There were emotions there that the five-year-old Catherine could almost choke on, but could not understand.

Generally, though, Catherine's life was happy. She did well at school and at home she was spoilt by her family, who encouraged her to sing and dance for them in the evenings on the rug in front of the fire. She was imaginative and loved stories. When she learned to read, as she did very quickly, John McMullen – who was totally illiterate – would get her to read the daily paper to him. Rose was little better, so there were no books in the house. Catherine had to make do with comics when she could get hold of them and the big Victorian-style Christmas compendiums. One in particular, called the *Chatterbox*, was a favourite with Catherine and the stories inside would be read and reread for many months. They had improving titles such as 'A Brave Girl', 'A Gallant Rescue', 'A Good Man's Tenderness', as well as the more melodramatic 'Can it be True?' or the tragic tales of 'Motherless Children' and orphans. Fatherless children of the illegitimate variety didn't feature in its moralistic pages. Religion played a large part in Catherine's childhood. As Irish Catholics, the McMullen household was visited frequently by the priests. Old John boasted that he'd never been inside a church except for his baptism, but Rose went to Mass when she could and the priests were respected visitors. Catherine felt herself singled out for moral attention without knowing precisely why. By the age of seven she already knew that there was a mystery.

Then suddenly everything changed. Rose's health broke down. Her heart, weakened by years of poor nutrition and heavy physical work, began to fail. Kate had to give up her job and come home to look after the family. Now Catherine shared the double bed in the little bedroom with Kate. Rose and John slept on another double bed in the parlour and young Jack in the kitchen. Kate's resentment at having to come home was clear. It also meant less money coming into the house and Kate had to take in laundry and go out cleaning in order to make ends meet, as well as looking after her bedridden mother and the two men. Old John and young Jack were only intermittently in work as the pre-war slump put the dockyards into an even steeper decline. Catherine became aware of gender stereotypes at a very early age: the men, even when out of work and sitting idle in the chair before the fire, never lifted a finger to help in the house; in contrast Kate blacked the boots, carted coal, scrubbed floors, shopped, heaved tubs of water for the laundry, cooked, sewed and cleaned from six in the morning to ten o'clock at night. Even as a small child, Catherine felt contempt for the men.

But it wasn't only the domestic situation that changed dramatically. Catherine was playing with some of her friends in the street when there was a quarrel over ownership of some bits of broken china they were using in the game. Catherine threatened to 'tell her Da'. One little girl turned on her and said, 'He isn't your Da, he's your Granda. Your Kate's your Ma and you haven't got a Da.' The words were scorched into Catherine's consciousness for the rest of her life. She fled into the outside toilet and sat on the wooden seat, staring at the wall for a long time. When the pain had subsided and she had had time to think, Catherine realized that the girl's words solved some of the mysteries that she had sensed in the family relationships around her. When she came out of the toilet and stood looking at the back windows of the house, and saw Kate moving around in the kitchen, Catherine said that she looked at Kate and knew that it was true. Kate was her mother.

Catherine's relatives describe her as having been a difficult child. But given the circumstances and Catherine's strong personality it's hardly surprising. After this revelation nothing was said; Catherine kept her new knowledge to herself. At 10 William Black Street, the emotional tug of war between

Kate and Rose continued with Catherine at its centre. She later remembered odd little incidents that underlined her true parentage: being taunted as a bastard by children in the street; Kate talking to a school mistress when she moved Catherine to a different school, telling her that her real name wasn't McMullen, it was Fawcett. But the incident that made the biggest impression took place at a birthday party. One of her friends in the street was giving a party and all the children were invited. Catherine, although she hadn't received a formal invitation, assumed that she would be invited too. On the day of the party, even though Kate tried to discourage her, she insisted on being dressed in her best pinafore, with a ribbon in her hair, and went to the door of the house expecting to be allowed in. She had heard all her friends talking and laughing and there were going to be jellies and cakes and games. But the door remained shut, even though Catherine could see the children looking at her out of the window. In the end she knocked, and eventually her friend came down and said, 'My Mam says you can't come to my party, because you haven't got a Da.' The door was then shut in her face.

Catherine said much later that this was the second big rejection in her life. The first was her father's abandonment of her, but she excused this because she said that he had done it before she was born, before he knew her. This second rejection hurt, because it was more personal. These people knew her and were supposed to be her friends, but they were still turning her away. Catherine burned with shame and anger. It was one of the spurs that drove her – she would show them what she could do. She would show them all. So deeply did it bite, that when that same little girl came to one of her book signings in Newcastle forty years later and tried to speak to her, Catherine cut her dead.

To fill the gap left by this lack of a father, Catherine created fantasy father figures. One of them was the local doctor who had brought her into the world, and had saved her life. Catherine told several people that Dr McHaffie was her father. The children at school almost believed it when they saw her being given a lift to school in his car. This episode appears in her first novel *Kate Hannigan*, and again with a slightly different twist in *A Grand Man* – the first of the Mary Ann books. When not fantasizing about Dr McHaffie, Catherine created another father, putting together all the bits of information she had gleaned from eavesdropping on adult conversations. Her father was a gentleman. She imagined all the houses that Kate had talked about from her days in service and created a wonderful house for him. One day he would come back for her and take her away from all this poverty and ugliness to live in a beautiful environment.

Catherine found such fantasies very satisfying. When she was old enough to ask awkward questions the fantasy was enhanced even further. Her aunt Mary told her many different stories about the man called Alec who had come to the Ravensworth Arms: how he had dressed like a gentleman and carried a silver-topped cane like the Silver King in the music hall; how beautifully he had talked – not with an ugly Geordie accent. Catherine thought that Mary's stories had an element of malice in them – how could someone so cultured marry someone as rough as Kate, she implied? Mary gave other information too. She said that Catherine's father was the son of a big brewing family in Newcastle, and he liked going to the races. Catherine soaked up these little pieces of information and stored them away.

The hurt and anger that she felt spilled over into her relationship with her mother, whom she still called Kate. As time went on, trapped in a cycle of domestic drudgery and unimaginable poverty, Kate – still barely thirty – became

The streets of Jarrow.

increasingly depressed. One day, after a particularly hard slog, struggling with wet sheets, her hands raw from constant soaking in detergent, her back breaking from the heavy lifting of water buckets and laundry baskets, she told Catherine that she saw her life draining away 'like water down a dark alley'. She took to drink to anaesthetize her misery. Catherine hated her for it and their relationship became increasingly turbulent.

When Rose McMullen died, Catherine was deeply affected. This was the woman she had regarded as her mother for the first seven years of her life and to whom she had looked for the love and affection her real mother wasn't allowed to give. Catherine described in her autobiography how she was sleeping in the same room as her grandmother when she died. The decomposing corpse in the coffin on trestles in the parlour – Kate emptying the stinking buckets of fluid that drained from it – made a lasting impression.

From then on it was just Catherine and Kate, with her grandfather, Uncle Jack and a series of lodgers. Sarah and Mary were both married: Sarah was living in Birtley, Gateshead, but Mary was living in the same street as the McMullens. As she entered adolescence Catherine said that she became aware that Kate was the object of licentious advances by both her half-brother and her stepfather. This not only added to Catherine's confusion about sex, it also increased her contempt for men – the kind of contempt she describes in her novel *Justice is a Woman*, when her character declares that 'most women could buy a man at one end of the street and sell him at the other'. Her feelings were also fuelled by a more mature understanding of her father's behaviour towards herself and Kate. The teenage Catherine

31

began to ask more and more questions about the missing Alexander. Kate made it plain that she didn't want to talk about him, but Aunt Mary was more forthcoming. After all, Mary had been working at the Ravensworth Arms with Kate when Alexander had been courting her – they had shared a bedroom and certain confidences. So Catherine tried to find out as much as she could. The story of his visits, Kate's love for him, her unshakable belief that he would honour his promises, and her eventual betrayal were all laid out for Catherine, as well as the strange story of his visit to the house in Leam Lane.

Finding her father became an obsession, especially after Kate married one of the lodgers. David McDermott was a merchant seaman, one of two men who regularly stayed at Number 10 when on shore leave. He had been coming to the house since Catherine was six and had always made a fuss of her. When David's wife died in Ireland he asked Kate to marry him. Catherine was horrified and never accepted him as a stepfather. It fell to the sixteen-year-old to go down to the Register Office with the forms for Kate, and this visit, as well as the longing for her real father created by her mother's marriage, seems to have precipitated Catherine's search for her real identity.

At the Register Office she tried to find her birth certificate, but when she gave her names – both Catherine Fawcett and Catherine McMullen – and her date of birth of 20 June 1906, there was no entry that matched at all. Catherine came to the conclusion that, being illegitimate, she had no birth certificate. She went to elaborate lengths from then on to avoid having to produce it. There were still people alive in 1921 who had been born before the days of compulsory registration, so production of a birth certificate was not as mandatory as it is today. After failing in her attempt to see her birth certificate, Catherine went out in secret to Lamesley, to the Ravensworth Arms. Her Aunt Sarah lived at Birtley, only a few miles away, and Catherine regularly cycled over to see her, so it was a reasonably easy thing to do. But at the Ravensworth Arms, Catherine had difficulty finding anyone who had been there when her mother had worked at the pub. In the end she was directed to the blacksmith's wife, who had known Kate before she was married. Catherine went to the forge and enquired about the man who had courted her mother nearly twenty years earlier. She was apparently told that 'Alec' had been sacked by his employer subsequently and had 'gone south'. Whatever else she learned, she never told anyone.

Catherine had begun to go out with a couple of young miners she had met at the Catholic youth club. One of them, Kit Gannon, earned a bit of money working for a bookie on the side and Catherine entrusted him with the task of looking for her father. This suggests that at this point her Aunt Mary had at least told Catherine the name he had been known by. Catherine recklessly promised the lovelorn Kit that if he found Alexander for her, she would marry him. Some other details she had learned about her father must have prompted her to ask Kit to do this rather than anyone else. Maybe someone had told her that Alexander gambled, had a passion for the horses, and was a bookie too? Or had she caught wind of the fact that, in the early 1920s, ill and down on his luck, he was working in one of the mines in County Durham? It is impossible to know. Whatever happened, Kit didn't find anything out at all, so Catherine was never in any danger of having to honour her promise.

Despite going out with Kit and another young miner, Micky Moran, Catherine – now aged about twenty – was in the grip of unrequited love for an older man. He was an insurance agent who sat in front of her at Mass and barely noticed her existence, and was in fact going out with someone else. After two years of worshipping him from a distance, one glorious day he spoke to her as they left the church and Catherine walked home several feet above the ground. He began to take her dancing, or to the cinema, though he never kissed her or held her hand or made any of the gestures of affection that she might have expected from a boyfriend. After more than a year of this, she became increasingly distressed. He seemed to go to great lengths not to be seen with her publicly. When they went on holiday together to a religious retreat centre near Gilsland in Cumbria, he insisted that they arrive separately. She invited him to her staff Christmas Ball at the Harton Workhouse, where she worked as a laundry checker, but he didn't turn up. The same thing happened when she invited him to the twenty-first birthday party her aunt Mary arranged for her. There were excuses, but Catherine saw through them. She knew that he was ashamed of her. She wasn't good enough for him. Illegitimate, uneducated, brought up in the New Buildings, she didn't fit into his scheme of self-advancement. It made Catherine very bitter. This, she said later, was the third rejection, and the most hurtful of them all: 'Because this man knew me, and he knew how much I loved him, and he still rejected me.'

More determined than ever to 'show them', Catherine now applied for and got the job of laundry manageress at a work-house in Essex. It was a considerable promotion for a girl so young, and it also meant going south, where she believed her father to be. She still hoped that one day they would meet and he would recognize her. The fantasy of the 'gentleman' was still intact and she was determined to behave like a gentleman's daughter. She bought beautiful clothes, either second-hand or by paying for them on a weekly basis. She went to elocution lessons, tried to learn French and to play the violin. More importantly she discovered the letters of Lord Chesterfield, written in the eighteenth century to his illegitimate son, giving him instruction and education, and they became Catherine's bible. She read the books he recommended to his child, and tried to absorb all the – very

Workers at Harton Workhouse Laundry.

outmoded – social advice he gave. From Lord Chesterfield she learned that if she wanted to be a lady she would have to cultivate 'a distinguished politeness, an almost irresistible address, a superior gracefulness in all you say or do. It is this alone can give all your other talents their full lustre and value.' Where her father learned his charm and irresistible address we will never know – it was probably innate. For Catherine the conventions of social intercourse had to be learned and she believed that the rewards would be the popularity and social acceptance she craved. 'If you improve and grow learned everyone will be fond of you and desirous of your company,' Chesterfield promised. For months she read the thick volumes of letters and practised everything that was necessary to accomplish the transformation.

When she left Jarrow on the train for her new life in the south, Catherine thought herself every bit the lady she felt herself to be. She confessed, later in life, that she was acting out a part, trying to become someone she was not.

3

THE MISSING
BIRTH CERTIFICATE

People in Jarrow had treated Catherine's social pretensions – her need to better herself – with ridicule. They regarded her as an 'upstart'. In Essex no one knew her background and she was taken at face value – until the arrival of Annie Joyce, a young laundress from the Harton workhouse in Jarrow, put an end to that. Annie saw no reason to keep Catherine's history secret and soon everyone at the laundry knew she was illegitimate, and that her family were uneducated and poor. Catherine's anger was monumental: she didn't speak to her again for more than thirty years. Catherine immediately began applying for other jobs and soon found herself managing an even bigger laundry at the workhouse in Hastings. Here, she thought, she could finally leave the past behind. But soon the workhouse matron began asking for her birth certificate and Catherine was forced to admit that she didn't have one. The matron gently pointed out that everyone of her age, even those who were illegitimate, had a birth certificate and advised Catherine to write to her mother.

CARLISLE PARADE AND PIER HASTINGS

The sea front at Hastings.

Swallowing her pride, Catherine wrote to Kate and received, almost by return of post, a birth certificate that had been scribbled on and altered, but whose original words were still legible. With it was a letter from Kate, running to several pages, telling her that of course she had a father and that his name appeared on her birth certificate. Kate gave her some of the information she had longed to have. Now, for the first time, Catherine discovered that her real name was Catherine Ann Davies and her father was Alexander Davies – though he was not a commission agent, Kate explained, as she had put on the certificate. Receiving this information was a very emotional moment for Catherine, and it wasn't long before she was blaming her mother for withholding it, and building another barrier to the development of their relationship.

Nevertheless, Catherine and her mother patched things up, as they always did, and eventually Catherine invited Kate down to Hastings to live. Kate's husband was away at sea for long periods and she was lonely. Catherine rented a bigger flat and together they ran a boarding house. Then Catherine bought the Hurst, a fourteen-bedroom 'gentleman's residence', which Kate and Catherine's friend Nan Smyth ran while Catherine was out at work earning the money for the mortgage.

Owning the Hurst was very important for Catherine. It signalled that she had arrived. To own any house at all would have been an achievement, but fourteen bedrooms, a butler's pantry and a tennis court meant that she had the status she had always craved, even if the house was packed with lodgers to pay for it. Yet things did not go smoothly, and Kate soon had to leave because of disagreements, some of them violent. Her drinking had become a serious problem and it was decided that she and her daughter would be better apart.

Kate moved into the flat they had all occupied before the purchase of the Hurst and took in lodgers there to cover the rent. One of those lodgers was Tom Cookson, recently graduated from Oxford University and newly employed as a maths master at Hastings Grammar School for boys. Although he'd been to Oxford, Tom too came from a working-class background in Essex. His father had died when he was a small child and his mother had remarried. There was an immediate attraction between Tom and Catherine, complicated by the jealousy of Catherine's friend and companion Nan Smyth. Eventually Catherine had to buy Nan a house of her own to run as a lodging house in order to compensate her for the years of work she had contributed to the success of the Hurst.

Kate, too, caused problems and eventually Catherine persuaded her to return to the north-east and her husband.

In June 1940 Tom and Catherine were finally able to get married at St Mary's Star of the Sea in Hastings. For the first time Catherine was obliged to use the name on her birth certificate. She is described on her wedding certificate as Catherine Ann Davies, otherwise known as McMullen, the daughter of Alexander Davies, deceased. Whether Kate thought him dead because she had not heard from him for so long, or whether this was a convenient fiction to explain his absence to the priests, it is impossible to know. Catherine said she felt strange, almost fraudulent, using the name that had never been hers. Her true legal name as Kate Fawcett's illegitimate daughter

Catherine writing Our Kate.

doesn't appear; she had never used it, having been known all her life by her grandparents' name. Long afterwards Catherine talked about her joy in finally having a surname that truly belonged to her – she was legitimately Mrs Catherine Cookson. 'I was so grateful to Tom,' she said, 'for giving me a name.'

The war was a very difficult time for Catherine. Depression aggravated by the stillbirth of her first baby and four subsequent miscarriages escalated into a full-scale breakdown. She was admitted to a mental hospital in Herefordshire where she endured a series of ECT treatments which left her with an impaired memory. This did not stop her writing, however. She had begun to write stories and plays, mostly about the rich, landed gentry who fascinated her, but whose daily lives she knew nothing about. This absence of real knowledge meant that her work was stilted and lacked narrative drive, her characters had little depth and the dialogue was unreal. People who read her work – a literary lodger at the Hurst and later the Hastings writers' circle – confirmed that they weren't good enough to publish and some of them were awful. But Catherine persevered, though her efforts were hindered by her mental state – which was still delicate. The rejections and traumas of her childhood burned in her mind as if they had been newly inflicted. And then one night, in a fit of depression, she described how a little girl came out from behind the mirror – a little girl who looked suspiciously like Kitty McMullen. The child asked why Catherine didn't write about her? And Catherine saw, straight away, that writing about the child she had been and what she had suffered might be a way out of her depression. She could write it all out of herself and be healed. The biggest rejection of all, because it was the cause of all the other rejections, was her illegitimacy – the failure of her father to come back and make her legitimate. And so her first story was entitled 'The Girl Who Had No Da'. Its success among the members of the Hastings writers' circle encouraged Catherine to write more in the same vein.

Her first novel, *Kate Hannigan*, is about a young woman who has an illegitimate child Annie, and is transparently auto-biographical. The local doctor who delivers the child, saving both their lives, becomes the hero of the book, falling in love with Kate and eventually, after many trials and tribulations which include losing a leg in the First World War, he marries her. John Smith, the agent to whom she sent the book, was impressed from the beginning by the freshness of the writing and the directness of her style. It came straight off the page and into the heart of the reader. The fact that it didn't fit into any of the usual genres was a bit of a stumbling block, but Macmillan Publishers were willing to take a risk on it.

In 1953 Kate, whose husband had died in a tragic accident a few years earlier, was discovered to have incurable cancer of the stomach. Catherine immediately decided that she would nurse her mother through her final illness and brought her down from South Shields to Hastings. But it wasn't just that she wanted to repair her relationship with her mother before she died – she confessed that there were a number of important questions she needed to have answered. She wanted to talk to Kate and find out as much as she could about her father before it was too late. Surely Kate, who had previously been reticent about details, could have no scruples now and would be willing to tell all? That these conversations did take place, Catherine admits freely, but she has never said what it

*Catherine, Tom and their poodle Sandy standing in the doorway
of their home in Northumberland.*

was that Kate told her. But it's significant that after Kate's death in 1956 Catherine, although she had the money and the resources, never admitted to having made any attempt to trace her father – which she could quite easily have done. Publicly she lamented his absence from her life – even saying in interviews that she would love to know who he was and to meet his family, the family she had never known. Privately she persisted with the fantasy of the gentleman stranger. Whatever Kate had told her, Catherine now knew enough about her father to know that she didn't want to go in search of him. He wasn't worth finding.

Catherine, meanwhile, poured all her confused feelings about her mother into a novel – one of the few she wrote that is in the first person – and it is a brave attempt to get 'inside' her mother's mind and try to imagine what it must have been like to be her. Christine, Catherine said afterwards, was her mother as she imagined she might have been. *Fenwick Houses* is one of Catherine's best novels: Christine is beautiful and sensitive, but has the misfortune to be born into a family riven by poverty and violence. She, like Kate, allows a well-spoken handsome young man to make love to her and bears an illegitimate child. Attempts to find him afterwards are thwarted by the fact that she only knows half his name. Worn down by misery, Christine takes to drink.

A few years afterwards, Catherine wrote *The Gambling Man*, about a handsome young man with upwardly mobile social ambitions and an eye for the ladies, who earns a lot of money on the side by gambling and ends up bigamously married (though through no fault of his own) to two women at the same time. This could be just coincidence, but it seems strange that Catherine should write such a plot just after she had talked to Kate about her father. The swaggering ladies man, the gambling and the bigamy sum up her own father's life – for Alexander was not the gentleman of her imagination. The truth, when finally uncovered, was quite different. It is ironic that Catherine's father, the real Alexander Davies, could become a character she created for one of her novels, his life story as complicated and interesting as any Cookson hero.

Only once did Catherine admit that she knew who he was. In a television interview for Tyne Tees she told the interviewer that, yes, she did know, but that the information would go to the grave with herself and Kate. In another interview the closest she ever came to admitting that the 'gentleman father' was a fantasy was when she said that 'We illegitimates never choose an ordinary man as a father, a bus conductor or a labourer – it always has to be someone special'.

One result of the mystery with which she surrounded her parentage was that she had people writing in all the time claiming to be related to her. On one occasion a particular family appeared to have most of the details right, except that, when Catherine looked more closely, the individual they proposed would have been a small child at the time of her birth. Her real family, the family she chose not to know, never wrote to her, although they were certain that there was a connection. There were too many coincidences – a name in common, physical likeness, as well as geographical proximity. The thought that she might think they had simply come with a begging bowl, or the fear that she might actually reject them, deterred them from coming forward.

There was one other reason why Catherine's real nieces and nephews were convinced they were related to her. Apart from the shame of illegitimacy, Alexander had passed on another legacy to Catherine – something hidden in her genetic code from the day she was conceived. Catherine had begun to suffer from nose bleeds when she was a teenager, and as she grew older they became more frequent and intense. Her mouth too began to bleed. She lived with the inconvenience and the debilitating effects of copious haemorrhages that continued despite numerous attempts to cauterize the blood vessels. In middle age, as well as severe anaemia, she noticed brown spots appearing on the skin of her face. Doctors had always dismissed her complaints – nose bleeds were common and not life-threatening. But on this occasion, when she sought medical advice, expecting the same dismissive treatment, she saw a young locum GP, newly qualified, who recognized the brown rings as symptoms of a rare and serious condition and referred Catherine to a consultant in London. There she was questioned and examined in front of a group of medical students. Had her mother or any members of her mother's family suffered from nose bleeds, he asked? Catherine was able to tell him that they did not. What about her father's family? Hot with humiliation, Catherine was forced to admit that she was illegitimate and that she didn't know anything about her father. Still burning with the shame of this public confession, Catherine scarcely took in the implications of what the consultant then told her. She had an inherited disease called hereditary haemorrhagic telangiectasis, or HHT, usually passed on from parent to child. Since her mother didn't have it, it must have come from her father.

Rogue blood vessels grew in the mucous membranes through-out the body, particularly the nose and digestive tract – sometimes even the lungs – and periodically they would haemorrhage. Pints of blood could be lost at a time, and it was incurable. Catherine was devastated.

4

THE SEARCH
FOR ALEXANDER

When I began my search for Catherine's lost father I had only a few pieces of information to go on. The only facts I knew for certain were that he had been in the north-east in 1905 and 1906 and suffered from hereditary haemorrhagic telangiectasis. He had been known – at least to Kate – as Alexander Davies, but Kate had inferred that there was a question mark over the surname. There was also the Fawcetts' description of him to go on: the handsome man in a black coat with an astrakhan collar and a silver-topped cane with a slightly theatrical air; someone who didn't speak with a Geordie accent, though he had connections in Newcastle, and who may well have moved south after the affair with Kate. This was all very vague and circumstantial. I also thought that he might well have been married – which would explain his inability to honour his promises. Kate had hinted that she knew he wasn't free to marry her, and the woman who opened the door of the house in Newcastle and denied him to Rose and Kate sounded suspiciously like an aggrieved wife. But there could have been many other reasons why he had abandoned her. If he really had been a gentleman, then his family wouldn't have been too keen on his marriage to a barmaid from the rough end of Jarrow. A hundred years ago, these things mattered even more than they do now.

After the publication in 1969 of Catherine's autobiography, *Our Kate*, there was a lot of speculation about Alexander's identity. Many people, disbelieving Catherine's fantasies of a gentleman father, cynically asserted that it was probably one of the servants at Ravensworth Castle, where Kate had worked and where, according to gossip, she had caught the eye of the butler. One journalist actually published a group photograph of the servants taken in the grounds of the castle, posing the question 'Is Catherine Cookson's father here?' The following day he had a telephone call from Catherine herself, incandescent with rage. 'My father is not in that photograph,' she insisted. In London publishing circles, people speculated about her step-grandfather John McMullen, who had brought her up as his daughter and was much loved by Catherine. He was also known to have made sexual advances to Kate. I listened to the gossip, but kept an open mind. I didn't feel that Catherine would have written about him with such warmth, or regarded him with such a deep affection, if she had been the product of incest. Nor did I think Kate devious enough to have invented an Alexander Davies in order to conceal the father's real identity. The late registration, the pathetic lie that she was his wife, only made sense if done in a fit of desperation, after waiting in vain for the return of the real Alexander Davies. Kate had told Catherine categorically that that was the name she had known him by. Then there were all the stories from the family members who knew the circumstances. These all pointed to the existence of Alexander as a real individual. Nor did any of these stories fit with speculation that Catherine's father was an aristocrat or a foreigner, perhaps even a Belgian Count visiting Ravensworth Castle. However, if I was going to make any progress, I would have to take all these stories and investigate them in order to prove that they were false trails.

I looked at all the records for Ravensworth Castle, including lists of servants. None of the names or descriptions fitted. I even checked for guests, or business associates of Lord Ravensworth who might have visited the castle during this period. It was a busy time – two earls died one after the other and there were two dowager countesses arguing about owner-ship of jewellery and furniture. One of them scandalized the family by marrying her footman; another returned to her own family in Devon. Among all those toing and froing from London and the West Country was a lawyer called Walter Davies Bewes. Here was the name Davies, and double-barrelled, as Catherine had hinted in her novel *Fenwick Houses*. Had Walter a son called Alexander who might have travelled to the Castle on his father's business? But directories, electoral rolls and the St Catherine's Index of Births, Marriages and Deaths failed to reveal such a person. There was also an insurance agent called Davies, from Barnard Castle in county Durham, but no member of the family called Alexander. I had drawn a blank and with the deadline for the delivery of the biography already past, I had to leave the search in order to finish it.

Over the next few months I began to think about it more and more. Detective stories have always fascinated me and this was a particularly tricky one to solve. There was so little evidence – just a name and a hereditary disease. What chance did I have of finding him? Realistically very little. Common sense told me that it wasn't worth my time. But I couldn't forget it. Soon, every time I had to be in the library, I began to spend an hour or two looking at records. My partner had begun to trace his family history and I sometimes went with him and, while he looked for his great-grandparents, I looked for Alexander Davies. In any genealogical search, the St Catherine's Index is an invaluable resource. It lists the births, deaths and marriages of everyone in England and Wales since registration became compulsory in 1837. Each microfiche covers several letters of the alphabet, with dozens and dozens of pages on each fiche, every page containing scores of entries. I became very familiar with the quirky irreverences of the Index, searching often between Cal to Fog and Bro to Egg. Eventually I became expert at guessing the exact spot on each fiche where the name Davies would be. Working on the knowledge that Alexander Davies had been in the north-east during the first decade of the twentieth century, I went right through the Index from 1900 onwards to see if there was any trace of him. Perhaps the reason he didn't come back to marry Kate was that he had died? Or, if he was a married man, there might be a record of his marriage. I found surprisingly few entries for 'Alexander Davies', even allowing for variations in spelling. It isn't a particularly common combination of names in England, which is lucky, since copies of certificates cost six pounds fifty each and I had to order one for every mention of a person with the right name in order to get the maximum information. Birth certificates give parents' names, addresses and occupations. Marriage certificates are most useful since they give the ages of the bride and bridegroom, their occupations and addresses, as well as their fathers' names and occupations and the names of two witnesses who are often family members as well. The first reference I found was an Alexander Davies who had married a widowed lodging housekeeper in 1903, but when the certificate arrived he was an elderly sea captain and there was no suggestion at any time that Catherine's father had been a very old man – quite the opposite. Then I found that an Alexander Davies had married in Darlington in December 1909, so I sent for this certificate too and it yielded some very interesting details. This particular Alexander was thirty-four, a drapery traveller living at 12 Park Place in Darlington, and his father was a horsedealer, also called Alexander Davies. His bride was twelve years older, a forty-six-year-old widow called Jane Williamson, living at the same address. Something about this certificate aroused my curiosity. Perhaps it was the mention of horses – Kate's Alexander had enjoyed going to the races, or perhaps it was his occupation. A drapery traveller would have had ample reason to go to the Ravensworth Arms to sell linen and his visits would have been irregular. Travelling 'reps' were also very well dressed. But if this was the man, why would he have married a woman so much older than himself, only three years after Catherine's birth, when he had the option of marrying someone as young and attractive as Kate, especially as he had claimed to be so much in love with her? I needed to know more about this Alexander, if only to eliminate him from the search.

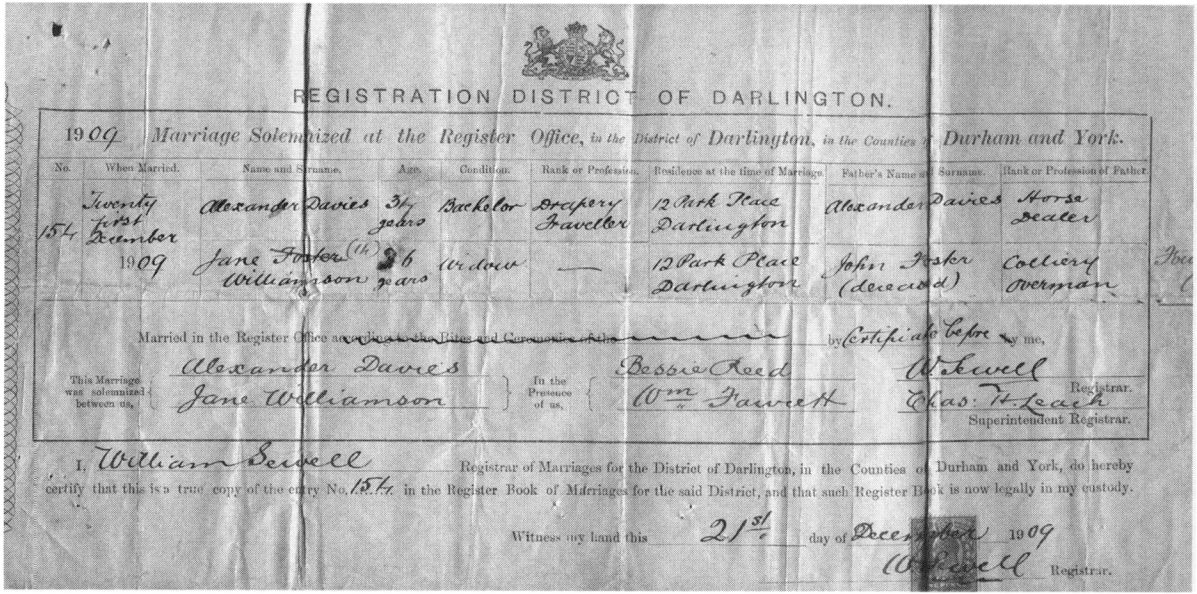

REGISTRATION DISTRICT OF DARLINGTON.

1909 Marriage Solemnized at the Register Office, in the District of Darlington, in the Counties of Durham and York.

No.	When Married.	Name and Surname.	Age.	Condition.	Rank or Profession.	Residence at the time of Marriage.	Father's Name and Surname.	Rank or Profession of Father.
154	Twenty first December 1909	Alexander Davies	31 years	Bachelor	Drapery Traveller	12 Park Place Darlington	Alexander Davies	Horse dealer
		Jane Foster (formerly) Williamson	26 years	Widow	—	12 Park Place Darlington	John Foster (deceased)	Colliery Overman

Married in the Register Office according to the Rites and Ceremonies of the ~~Established Church~~ by Certificate before me,

This Marriage was solemnized between us, Alexander Davies, Jane Williamson. In the Presence of us, Bessie Reed, Wm Fawcett.

W. Sewell Registrar.
Chas. H. Leach Superintendent Registrar.

I, William Sewell Registrar of Marriages for the District of Darlington, in the Counties of Durham and York, do hereby certify that this is a true copy of the entry No. 154 in the Register Book of Marriages for the said District, and that such Register Book is now legally in my custody.

Witness my hand this 21st day of December 1909

W. Sewell Registrar.

Alexander's marriage certificate.

From the marriage certificate of this Alexander Davies it seemed that he had been born sometime in 1875, but public records aren't always trustworthy: people lie, officials make mistakes, or mishear information. The St Catherine's Index had already been copied by hand three times by the time it got onto microfiche. Sometimes when records are copied, handwriting is misread, names and dates are altered. So with this in mind, I looked through birth records not only for 1875, but a few years on either side. There were surprisingly few: only seven for the crucial year and I sent for every certificate. But not a single Alexander had a father called Alexander. There were two local babies with the right name, both born to men who worked in the big steel mills of county Durham. But of these two, one died as a child and the other moved with his family back to Wales. There was also a Welsh Alexander who at first looked promising. He was the posthumous son of a merchant seaman, brought up by his Irish mother in Cardiff, eventually becoming a seaman himself. The merchant marine seemed fertile ground, since it allows mobility. The Tyne was a huge, working port and it was quite possible that Catherine's father had come originally as a seaman and settled there. For a while he was my frontrunner, even though his father's name wasn't Alexander. There are lots of reasons why people lie about their family details. But it became clear that the Welsh Alexander was unlikely. A few years later he had taken a shore job as barman in a pub, married a local farmer's daughter and, during the period when he should have been in the north behaving badly, was at home fathering babies by his wife.

Perhaps Alexander hadn't been born in England or Wales? Alexander and its diminutive 'Alec' are very common in

Scotland and there are a lot of Scots in the Newcastle area. Scottish records are available on the internet at the Scots Origins website, so I checked out all the entries for Alexander Davies or Davis born in Scotland. Of the relevant entries, one was re-registered a month later as a girl, and two died in childhood, leaving only one that could possibly be a candidate, and for a while I thought I had struck gold. There was an Alexander Davis, son of Alexander Davis – not a horse-dealer, but an Irish labourer from Donegal, working in the Glasgow docks. The family seemed to have been widely travelled, as according to the Census, the eldest child had been born in America. The youngest, Alexander, was exactly the right age. But further research indicated that this Alexander too had remained firmly grounded in the Glasgow area and there was no evidence that he had ever visited the north-east of England at all. When Alexander Davies was getting married in Darlington, Alexander Davis was rooted in Glasgow. Although both had been born in the same year and had a father called Alexander, they didn't seem to be the same man. It was all very puzzling.

Although today it would be comparatively easy for a man living in Glasgow or Cardiff to father a child in Newcastle and scarcely be missed from home, at the beginning of the twentieth century people didn't travel casually as they do today. In 1905, most local travel was still by horse-drawn vehicle. Few people in Britain – only the very rich – had a car and they didn't go very far in them as they were still slow, uncomfortable and unreliable. Cars were just expensive toys rather than a means of travel, requiring a man to walk in front of them carrying a flag. If people had to go any distance from home, they travelled by rail. This, however, was very expensive and beyond the reach of most working-class people. If they had to go anywhere, perhaps to visit a relative, they travelled by walking, or hitching lifts with horse-drawn carriers' carts over larger distances. To go anywhere outside your local area took a long time and in those days, if you were working, there was very little time off. Domestic servants often had only one halfday a week. Factory operatives and miners might have Sunday as a day of rest. Holidays were only for the wealthy middle classes. There were few employers willing to give paid holiday to their workers: the idea of an annual holiday is a relatively recent development. So if Catherine's father was an ordinary working man, it was pretty certain that he must have been living locally at the time he was in contact with her mother, or been rich enough, or had the kind of job that would have enabled him to travel to and from the north-east. A labourer in the Glasgow docks didn't fit any of these criteria – nor did it match the family description of Catherine's father.

The next step was to check the records in Ireland. There were only four babies born in Ireland with that name during the critical period and none of them turned out to be a possibility. Then another thought occurred to me – if this Alexander was the son of a horsedealer, was it possible that his family had been itinerant? Perhaps he hadn't been registered at all. There were many families in the late nineteenth century who neglected to register their children's births. Or could he have lied about his father's name and identity? If he had been illegitimate, like Catherine, his birth certificate might bear a different name. His mother might even have remarried and taken her new husband's name for herself and her child. If this was the case, the likelihood of my tracking him down was very slim. The search was becoming increasingly daunting, but by now it had also become compulsive. I was now spending more and more time looking for Alexander's birth certificate and had even enlisted the help of my partner so that we could double the number of records searched in the same time.

At this point I discovered that the 1881 Census was available on CD-Rom not only in the central libraries, but could also be purchased. I sent away for it and began spending my evenings making lists of every Alexander Davies/Davis in Britain mentioned on the Census. If he was born before 1881, he was probably on it somewhere. All the babies whose births I had already discovered were listed, or, if they had died, their families and siblings were there. But it confirmed what I had already established: apart from my Scottish labourer, there was no Alexander, son of an Alexander, born in 1875 or the years either side of it. It seemed that he simply did not exist before his marriage in 1909. I even checked for foreign births to British Nationals, including those on military service, but there were none. Then I looked at all the foundling hospitals and workhouses on the Census for children called Alexander who matched his age, but also drew a blank. Of the illegitimate children called Alexander who might have adopted the surname Davies as an adult, only one was the right age, and because he was born on a farm the idea that his unnamed father might have been a horsedealer seemed to make him a hopeful choice. But later research ruled this man out too. I had drawn a complete blank.

For a couple of months I did nothing. I was tired of spending long afternoons in the library staring at a microfiche reader, deciphering small print, on what seemed an impossible task. Then a thought began to grow. Having failed to track down Alexander's birth, it occurred to me that I might be able to find a record of his death. So I began again the slow, systematic and very tedious job of going through the records of deaths from 1910 onwards, searching for any Alexander Davies whose age at death matched that of the man whose marriage certificate I possessed. Men who died in the First World War are also listed on the internet and I checked out every likely candidate, in case he had been killed in battle, but it was a fruitless search.

Year after year, box after box of microfiches, I ploughed painstakingly on, listing the death and age of every Alexander Davies I could find. My partner entered them onto a computer spreadsheet and the computer then calculated which death fitted which birth. I gradually built up a dossier of every Alexander Davies who had lived and died between 1860 and 1950. I found very few with obvious links to the north-east, and none of these had a father called Alexander or were recorded as suffering from HHT when they died. There were many false trails. One was a man in his mid-fifties, who had died in Tendring in Essex – the very place that Catherine had gone to for her first job when she left the north-east. Hadn't Catherine once been told that her father had lost his job and 'gone south'? It took a couple of weeks to trace this particular Alexander and his wider family, but it was soon apparent that he was a greengrocer from the East End of London who had developed cirrhosis of the liver and gone to Tendring to be nursed by his niece. Fifty-four when he died in 1914, his age and other details matched neither that of the Alexander, son

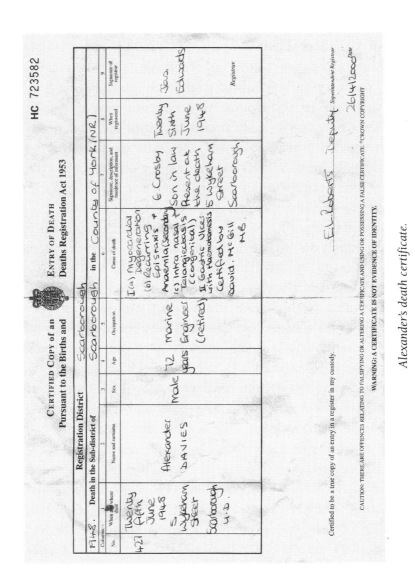

HC 723582

CERTIFIED COPY of an
Pursuant to the Births and

ENTRY OF DEATH
Deaths Registration Act 1953

Registration District Scarborough

Death in the Sub-district of Scarborough **in the** County of York (NR)

1948.

No.	When and where died	Name and surname	Sex	Age	Occupation	Cause of death	Signature, description, and residence of informant	When registered	Signature of registrar
427	Twenty Fifth June 1948 5 Wykeham Street Scarborough U.D.	Alexander DAVIES	Male	72 years	Marine Engineer (retired)	I(a) Myocardial Degeneration (b) Recurring Epistaxis + Anaemia (secondary) (c) Intra nasal Telangiectasis (congenital) II Gastric Ulcer with Haematemesis Certified by David. McGill M.B.	G Crosby Son in law Present at the death 5 Wykeham Street Scarborough	Twenty Sixth June 1948	Jca Edwards Registrar.

Certified to be a true copy of an entry in a register in my custody. ........E.L. Roberts Deputy *Superintendent Registrar* 26/4/2000 *Date*

CAUTION: THERE ARE OFFENCES RELATING TO FALSIFYING OR ALTERING A CERTIFICATE AND USING OR POSSESSING A FALSE CERTIFICATE. ©CROWN COPYRIGHT
WARNING: A CERTIFICATE IS NOT EVIDENCE OF IDENTITY.

Alexander's death certificate.

of Alexander, I was looking for, or the man who had courted Kate; and he didn't appear to have travelled any further north than Essex throughout his life.

Three months later I had got to 1947 and still hadn't found the drapery traveller. I was beginning to become despondent and ready to admit that in spite of all my hard work, it really was an impossibility. And anyway, even if I did find this man, how was I going to know whether he was Catherine's father, rather than any of the other Alexanders I'd found? I had almost given up when, in the records for 1948 I found the death of a man in Scarborough who had been born in 1875. The age was right and the location augured well – many people from the north-east retired to Scarborough – but even so, after so many disappointments, I sent away for the certificate without much hope.

Two days later the death certificate was sent to me. I will never forget the feeling of elation when I opened the envelope. This man, of exactly the right age to be the drapery traveller from Darlington, had bled to death as a result of suffering from hereditary haemorrhagic telangiectasis. He also had the heart condition that Catherine herself developed in old age.

At last I had a man with the right name, a sufferer from HHT, with a connection to the north-east. The only hiccough was that his occupation was described as 'marine engineer'. Had he changed his job in the intervening years? His death had been registered by a son-in-law, a Mr George Crosby, which seemed to indicate that he had a daughter, and there was an address – 5 Wykeham Street, Scarborough. I was going to have to go down to Yorkshire and see what I could find there.

5

ALEXANDER'S DAUGHTER

Scarborough is a seaside town full of the echoes of past glories. The gothic, domed edifice of the Grand Hotel dominates the sea front, where once there was a fashionable spa. Now, around the arc of sand that forms the main beach, there are the usual cafés and amusement arcades and knick-knack shops found on almost every sea front, and at the end of the bay a small fairground with roundabouts and a big wheel, a shooting gallery and candyfloss stall. As the traditional English seaside holiday has declined, so has Scarborough. It's all rather run down and there's a lot of poverty and unemployment in certain areas, but in the 1930s, when Alexander Davies moved there, it was still a fashionable, thriving resort.

It was a cold, spring day when I arrived in Scarborough. I was due to do a broadcast on local radio and decided to combine it with a visit to the local library and record office to check the electoral rolls. Scarborough library, I discovered, had a very well-equipped local family history section, which contained the electoral records back to the 1930s. I began with the year 1948, the year Alexander died, checking the address on the death certificate to see who else was living in the house. And there was Alexander Davies, together with George Crosby – the man who had described himself as a son-in-law – and Mrs Jane Crosby, presumably Alexander's daughter. Going back through the records I found that he had lived there since the 1930s. His wife had died in 1945 and her name was also Jane, exactly the same as the drapery traveller's wife. My hunch that this was the same person appeared to be right. What puzzled me was this: if Alexander was the drapery traveller, according to the certificate his wife had been forty-six when they married and it seemed unlikely – though not impossible – that they would have had a child. Out of curiosity I began to check the electoral rolls forwards through time to see how long the Crosbys had continued to live in the house. To my amazement I discovered that they had lived there from Alexander's death to the present day. Such continuity is very rare in the second half of the twentieth century. George Crosby had died in 1998, but the current electoral roll showed that Alexander's daughter Jane was still alive and still at the same address. It seemed a tremendous stroke of luck and I felt very excited. Hopefully Jane would be able to give me the information I needed about the elusive Alexander, and perhaps she would even be able to solve the mystery of her father's missing birth certificate.

Wykeham Street is in the old part of Scarborough, a long terrace of small Victorian houses, all in the process of renovation into desirable family homes. Most still have the backyard and the outside toilet, though modern kitchen and bathroom extensions have been built. It's easy to imagine them as they once were. Number 5 bore all the signs of recent

5 Wykeham Street.

work: there were new double glazed windows and panelled doors, the paint on the outside of the house was clean and obviously recently applied. I knocked on the door but there was no reply. The next-door neighbour came to the door with her children and told me that the couple who owned it were at work. When I enquired about Mrs Crosby she told me that the old lady had died only a few months ago and the house had been sold and renovated. Seeing my obvious disappointment, she told me that a neighbour across the road, Roland X, had been a good friend and had looked after Mrs Crosby after her husband had died. He might be able to tell me more when he came back from work.

I felt very disappointed. I had missed Alexander's daughter by a matter of a few months. If only I'd started the search earlier. While I waited for Roland to come home, I decided to go to the cemetery and try to find the records for either burial or cremation for members of the family. The official there was very helpful, and as I had the dates of death for Alexander, his wife Jane and their daughter he rapidly found details of their funerals. Alexander and his wife had been buried, their daughter cremated, even though Alexander had purchased a plot for her. The official was able to give me a copy of the cremation order and on it was the name and address of Jane Crosby's daughter – Alexander's granddaughter – who was apparently living in America.

By now I was so caught up in the story that it didn't seem to matter whether this was anything to do with Catherine Cookson at all. I was fascinated by their lives and simply wanted to know their history. It was as if I had wandered inadvertently into a Cookson novel. We walked across the graveyard to the spot where Alexander was buried, only to discover that neither he nor his wife had a gravestone. There was only a blank stretch of grass with a number. No one seemed to have cared enough to erect a stone. Why?

Scarborough Cemetery.

I returned to Wykeham Street and rang Roland's doorbell. He was still in his working clothes but invited us in and made a cup of tea. He was a middle-aged man living on his own after a marriage break-up, who had befriended the equally lonely Jane Crosby across the street, who had been recently widowed. She had been a secretive, prickly woman, he said, someone who didn't encourage visitors; an eccentric who had refused to modernize the house – not even to the extent of having a bathroom or a telephone installed. George Crosby had been a quiet, kindly man who had worked on the buses. His nickname was Bing and he was liked by everyone, but ruled by his wife with a rod of iron. When Jane died, Roland said, the house was exactly as it had been when her father

Alexander had died. My heart sank as he described the bin liners full of letters and photographs that had been taken away to the tip by the people employed to clear the house.

When I drove back to Cumbria that night, I knew a great deal more about the Davies family, but was no nearer to finding out who Alexander really was or whether or not there was any connection with Catherine Cookson. The following morning I wrote a brief, discreet letter to Jane Crosby's daughter Kathy in America, saying only that I was tracing her family history for a book that I was working on and would be very interested in any information she could give me about her grandfather. I assured her that anything she told me would be totally confidential and hoped that she would be interested in knowing more about her family history. I posted the letter and waited, but there was a long silence. On the internet I looked up every person with the same name that I could find – there were several, including one with the address I had been given. There were also several email addresses for people with that name. I copied the letter to each of them by email, just in case the original letter had gone astray. But still there was no response.

I decided to approach the problem from a different angle. I sent for Jane Davies' death certificate and discovered that the age on it didn't match that of the drapery traveller's wife at all. She was twelve years younger. Had the original registrar made a mistake? If Jane had been thirty-four at the time of her marriage instead of forty-six it would explain how she came to have a daughter. Her birth certificate would tell me the truth, if I could find it. I knew from the marriage certificate that Jane had been married to someone called Williamson and that her previous name was Foster. I was beginning to realize why nationally funded research projects prefer to focus on men rather than women – the difficulty of tracing women through a number of name changes is not only expensive, but time-consuming. Knowing that there was a query about the year of Jane's birth, I began to look for a marriage, prior to 1909, of a Jane Foster to a man called Williamson. That would give me her age and a lot more family information. After many hours of searching, I found it. On 15 March 1890, in Auckland, county Durham, Jane Foster, aged seventeen, the daughter of a coal miner called John Foster, was married to the twenty-year-old Thomas Williamson, also a coal miner. Although Jane had signed her name confidently on her marriage certificate, her husband had put a cross, signifying that he was totally illiterate. The marriage had been witnessed by relatives Henry and Margaret Foster – giving me more names to help locate her.

The 1881 Census showed the Foster family living at Hunwick Lane Ends, county Durham – a large mining family. Jane was listed, alongside her age and place of birth, as well as her parents, six brothers and sisters and a lodger. A clear picture of the family began to emerge. Her father was a miner from Reeth in Yorkshire, and her mother came from South Shields – not far from where Catherine Cookson herself was born. The family's movements around the coal pits of county Durham were reflected in the places where their children were born – they had lived variously at Crook, Sunniside, Hunwick and Newfield.

Jane had been born at Sunniside – not the pretty country village its name suggests, but an ugly blackened mining

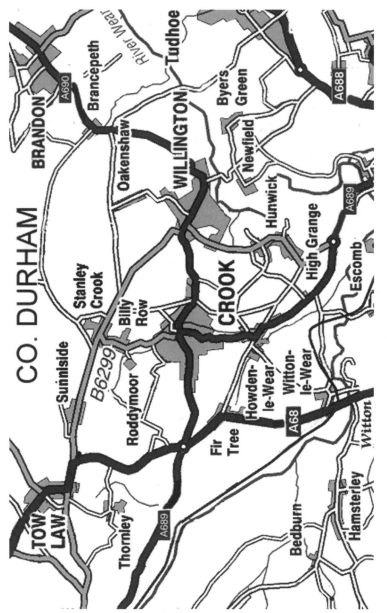

Map of the area, showing Newfield, Crook, Hunwick and Witton le Wear.

community surrounded by pit heads and slag heaps. Jane was the sixth of nine children, having two brothers and three sisters older than herself. According to her marriage certificate and the Census she should have been born in 1873 – a date which also matched the age on her death certificate. But when I went back to the St Catherine's Index to look for the registration of her birth, there was still a blank. I wrote to the registrar, outlining my problem and explaining why the research was important and received a letter and certificate by return of post. There had been more mistakes in the records. Jane's birth had been registered as Forster, not Foster – her mother, being illiterate, would not have detected the error. I wondered whether Jane had known about the Forster/Foster confusion and how she felt about having twelve years added to her age. When I was finally able to look at Jane's own copies of her birth and marriage certificates, she had angrily scribbled out the mistakes and corrected both her name and her age in bold black handwriting.

Armed with all this new information, I was able to trace other records relating to the family at the record office in Durham. In the 1891 Census for Newfield – the address on the marriage certificate – I found Jane, her first husband Thomas and a fourteen-year-old lodger, but no children of the marriage. They were living at 7 High Row, only a few doors away from Jane's parents at number 3. Other members of the extended Foster and Williamson families lived nearby in the long terraces of houses erected for the miners among the slag heaps and pit heads of Durham's busy coalfields. They didn't seem to have been church-goers, so their children had gone unchristened, and their marriages were civil affairs. But even if people never go to church in their lives, the one time they require the services of the priest is for the burial of the dead. I found the deaths of Jane's nieces and nephews – five of them all aged between three hours and nine years old – her brother, who had been killed in a mining accident, the premature deaths of her mother and father, their constitutions weakened by poor nutrition and heavy work. And eventually I found that of her first husband. In 1906, a few months after Catherine Cookson had been born, on an icy December day, Thomas Williamson, aged only thirty-six, died from pneumonia and exhaustion. Jane, a widow at thirty-three, in the days before the welfare state, lost her home – miners' houses were tied to the job – and had to find employment for herself. Like many women in a similar situation, she moved to Darlington, where the big weaving mills provided a living of sorts. She took lodgings in the town and there, two years later, she met a drapery traveller who worked for the Darlington firm of Richard Luck – Alexander Davies.

Going through the records of these small mining communities – the lists of houses and their occupants, their births, marriages and deaths – was a salutary experience: often fourteen or fifteen people were crammed into three rooms, sometimes three or four generations living together. The Censuses have to list how many rooms in the dwelling have windows and the figure is rarely more than two. Little wonder that their children died frequently, and the lifespan of an adult was about two-thirds of what we expect today. The men in particular died early from injury and coal-related illnesses, as well as heart disease. Many dropped down dead at the coal face. There was a temptation to be side-tracked into tracing other lives. Just along the street from Jane Williamson, two sisters married two brothers and lived in colliery houses side by side. Within a couple of months of each other, one sister had given birth to quads and the other to quins. How had they managed when medical technology was so primitive, I wondered? These babies were born at home, without the benefit of incubators, into families whose poverty can scarcely be imagined today. Three of the quins and one of the quads were baptized the day they were born and died a few days later, but the others seem to have survived for much longer. It was very tempting to trawl through the records to find out whether they reached adulthood, but I had to resist. One thing I did find out – the mother of the quads gave birth to another child only eleven months later. It made me very glad to have been born in the second half of the twentieth century!

I went to Newfield to look at the houses. It's a strange hamlet, perched on top of a hillside that still bears the scars of mining activity, only recently abandoned. The village itself remains very much a community, with a church and shop and isolated rows of houses with fantastic views out across county Durham. Although many of the rows have gone, High Row still exists, right at the top of the hill as its name suggests, a line of brick terraced houses stubbornly facing the north-easterly wind. Now the houses have double glazing and individually chosen front doors. The wash-houses and outside privies have gone and most of the backyards have been turned into tidy gardens. Number 3, where the young Jane Foster had lived with her family – eleven people in three rooms – had been modernized, like its neighbours, into a desirable residence. The house where seventeen-year-old Jane started married life with Thomas Williamson had been bulldozed down. A few years later, just before her husband died, she had moved back into 7 High Row. She belonged to a family that stayed very close together.

As well as finding out as much as I could about Jane Foster/Williamson/Davies' history, I had also sent away for

3 High Row, Newfield.

her daughter – Jane Crosby's – death certificate. I knew that this would give me her date and place of birth as well as the address of her surviving next of kin. Having now discovered the error about Jane Foster's age on her wedding certificate I was completely confident that this younger Jane would be her daughter – if not Alexander's – because it had occurred to me that Jane Foster Davies might already have had a daughter by her previous marriage, though I had never been able to find a record of any children to her and Thomas Williamson. You can imagine my consternation when Jane Crosby's death certificate arrived, stating that her maiden surname was neither Davies nor Williamson, but Smith. It was very mysterious. Could Jane Crosby have been married before? Fortunately the death certificate also gave me other useful information. Since the days of Alexander's death, it has become mandatory to include date and place of birth on death certificates – something that would have helped me enormously if it had been in place in 1948. Jane Crosby's date of birth was given as 8 June 1920 in Crook, county Durham.

I immediately began to trawl through the St Catherine's Index again, but I could find no record of a Jane Davies being born on that date anywhere in county Durham, and there were so many Jane Smiths it wasn't possible to know which might be the right one. So, in order to get more information, I sent away for her marriage certificate to George Crosby. I knew from the electoral rolls that it had to have taken place somewhere around 1948. The certificate confirmed this and it also told me that Jane was the daughter, not of Alexander and Jane Davies, but of a colliery overseer called Foster Smith

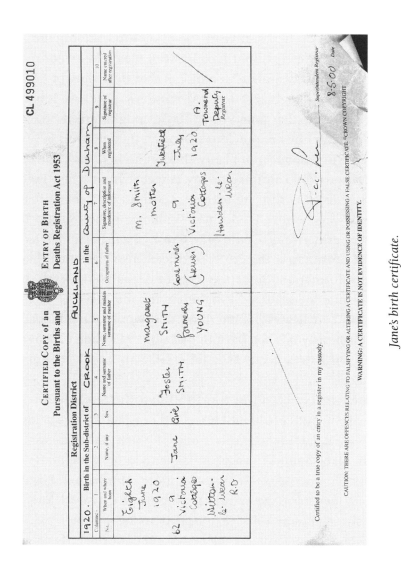

Jane's birth certificate.

who, according to the certificate, was still alive at the time of Jane's marriage to Alexander.

Once again I had to enlist the help of my indispensable registrar in Durham. I sent her Jane's date and place of birth and father's name and she sent me Jane's correct birth certificate. I discovered that she had been born at 9 Victoria Cottages, Witton le Wear, county Durham, the child of Margaret Young and Foster Smith. Far from clarifying things, this made the situation even more complicated. How had Jane come to be living with the Davieses, regarded by everyone as their daughter? Her husband George had described himself as a 'son-in-law' on Alexander Davies' death certificate. I was going to have to do a lot more research.

In Durham record office, I accessed the microfilms for the very limited electoral rolls available in 1920. At that time, people who rented houses, together with their wives or husbands, could be included in the rolls as well as property owners. My partner took one microfilm and I took the other and we began to look carefully through the tangled mining communities of the area for one particular address which was not listed in the index. I found nothing, but after about an hour he called me over and silently pointed to the image on the screen. There, rather blurred and blotchy was number 9 Victoria and the name of Foster Smith. There were also the names of three other people, who might be lodgers, and further down the page at the same address was the name Alexander Davies.

6

THE VICTORIA SEAM

The County Record Office in Durham has the full history of the ill-fated North Bitchburn Mining Company. It had some impressive shareholders, including one of the Queen Mother's relatives, the Hon. Charlotte Bowes Lyon, Lady Glamis. But the coal industry was already in decline at the beginning of the twentieth century, and small companies like the North Bitchburn lacked the resources to survive. Their flagging fortunes were temporarily halted by large government subsidies paid to mining companies during the First World War to raise production, and it was with one of these incentives that the company opened up a new seam at Witton le Wear called the Victoria Seam. They also built a whole row of new pit houses for the miners to live in. But it was not a profitable venture: the seam was thin and its proximity to the unpredictable Bitchburn Beck meant that there were problems with water leaking into the shafts and numerous roof collapses. It was a dangerous and unpleasant place to work. Nor was it well paid – basic pay was 24 shillings for a forty-eight-hour week.

Victoria was only one of a number of coal seams being worked in the area, a part of county Durham whose landscape had been changed in the nineteenth century from rolling hills and wooded river valleys, to slag heaps, railway lines, pit-head wheels, and smoking chimneys. A fire-clay pit and brick works were also operating in the valley and everything was covered in fine black coal dust which darkened the bricks of the buildings, clogged the lungs of the people who lived there, coated the leaves on the trees and speckled the washing hung out on lines in the backyards of hundreds of houses where the workers and their families lived. So many miners' houses were built that the streets weren't even named. Little bigger than rabbit hutches, the houses were erected either in long rows or square blocks and they were identified by a number, followed by the name of the pit, such as '8th Row Ashington, 4th Row Low Bitchburn, or Square 11, Newfield'. One such group is still known as 'the Fifty Houses'. Only one row was built at Witton for the new seam and it was simply called 'Victoria'. They were typical colliery houses: a kitchen and a living room downstairs, the largest room only about ten feet square, two tiny bedrooms upstairs, with a privy and wash-house outside in the backyard.

After the war ended in 1918, the Victoria Seam didn't last long. In 1921 the North Bitchburn Mining Company collapsed and was bought out by another firm who promptly closed the unprofitable workings. In January the employees received a fortnight's notice. Of 296 miners, only 84 were re-employed by the company. Finding out who these miners were was very difficult. Records reveal the social values of the employers at the time. Office staff – 'white collar workers' – are named and listed alongside their remuneration – even the tea boy has an identity – but of the men and boys who worked below ground there is not a mention. They are simply numbers on a worksheet – 24 hewers, 34 labourers, 6 pony boys, 4 firemen, 6 enginemen and so on. To find names for these men you have to look in the injury books which list accidents and illnesses and amounts of compensation paid out by the company to miners not fit to work. There can be found the true stories of the miners' lives: Joe Hudson, aged fourteen, pony boy, paid two shillings and sixpence because a coal tub ran over his foot; Mick McGann aged twenty-four, hewer, paid one shilling for a splinter of coal in his left eye; Tommy Young, aged eighteen, paid five shillings for having two fingers crushed between coal tubs, subsequently amputated; Jimmy Divock, hewer, thirty-two, paid sixpence in the fourteenth week after losing a leg in a roof fall; John McIntosh, labourer, forty-nine, paid his final sixpence after six months unable to work with 'bad lungs'. Many of the names recur: a year after the splinter in his eye, Mick McGann lost a finger in another accident. Very few of the miners escaped injury. By looking at the injury books and the electoral rolls for Victoria I was able to establish that Foster Smith, a hewer at the coal face, was kept on for a while. Alexander Davies, who seems to have been working as a labourer above ground, was not among those re-employed and moved away.

The most recent ordnance survey maps didn't show Victoria. What had been a thriving community in the 1920s seemed to have vanished off the face of the earth, and when I drove to Witton le Wear, now a pretty, rather gentrified village, there didn't seem to be any trace of its past history at all. There was a pub called the Victoria, with a long green trackway along the edge of the river valley to indicate where the railway had once been. Humps and mounds beside the river hinted at a fire-clay pit but the rows and rows of houses had all been demolished. The valley had gone wild again and there was little sign of the industrial hell created by the numerous mines, brick works and railway yards that polluted the landscape eighty years ago. But high up on the hill overlooking the valley, at High Grange, was a single block of back-to-back houses – still standing and still inhabited. There were children playing in the sheltered alleyway and pop music filtering out of open windows.

On the grass verge beside the road, an elderly man was feeding a collection of fantail pigeons. I asked him if he remembered the Bitchburn Mining Company and the Victoria Seam. He looked at me as if I had conjured up a ghost. 'Now that's a name I haven't heard in a long time,' he said. He thought for a while and scratched his head. Then he pointed down the valley towards Howden. 'Down there,' he said. 'Just along the road a bit and then off to the left.' He paused and then added, 'Fifty year ago you couldn't see up here for the chimneys and the conveyors and the slag heaps. But it's all gone now. And a lot of canny folk.' He sounded almost regretful.

Using the old man's recollections and a fifty-year-old map of the mine workings photocopied in the record office, we eventually found a rough track which began in the neighbouring village of Howden-le-Wear and swerved off in the direction of Witton. It was in poor condition and had enormous, water-filled pot-holes only navigable with local knowledge or a four-wheel drive. Driving very carefully, we came to a house named Victoria Cottage and beyond it a long, man-made level with one or two houses still standing at intervals beside the track. This is all that is now left of the Victoria Row – isolated dwellings where stubborn individuals held out against the demolition teams. Number 8 is still there and there is a small garden on the site of number 9. We stopped and took photographs, watched by a man mending a car and a couple of ponies swishing their tails beside the gate. The tiny 'two-up, two-down' house that had stood on this site had once held Alexander Davies and his wife Jane, the man called Foster Smith and his wife Margaret. It had also, according to the records, held three lodgers: Gertrude McAdam, Thomas Millar and Frank Ridley. I couldn't begin to imagine where

The site of 9 Victoria Row on the right.

they might all have slept. This was the house where Foster Smith's daughter Jane had been born and then mysteriously taken away by Alexander Davies and his wife. I still didn't understand why, and I needed to do much more research into her real father in order to uncover the truth.

Foster Smith is such an unusual name it didn't take long to comb the public records for births, deaths and marriages. There were three born in Yorkshire, but only one in the northeast and though he seemed the most likely, I couldn't be certain. I hesitated to pay for four birth certificates, only one of which would be correct, when I had – or thought I had – insufficient information to decide which of them would be the right one. I needed a marriage between Foster and Jane's mother Margaret Young to narrow it down. This entailed more long hours in the library looking at microfiches as I painstakingly worked my way back through the Smiths and Youngs. Soon I had another mystery. In 1912 the northeastern Foster Smith, a miner from county Durham, had married a girl called Elizabeth Young in Morpeth. A year later Elizabeth had a daughter called Olive, born at Maple Street in Morpeth on 8 June 1913. The next mention of a northeastern Foster was in 1920 when a daughter Jane Smith was born – the Jane I was looking for – and her date of birth was also 8 June. This seemed a strange coincidence. But Jane's mother was listed on her birth certificate as Margaret Young, not Elizabeth. Was this the same Foster Smith? If it was, there was an interval of eight years in which his wife had changed from Elizabeth to Margaret Young. Smith is one of the most common surnames in the St Catherine's Index and Elizabeth and Margaret two of the most common Christian names. Even after hours of trawling, and many fees wasted on incorrect certificates, I could still find no record of the death of an Elizabeth, or a marriage between Foster and Margaret. Were these women sisters? Did something happen to Elizabeth and did Foster subsequently live with Margaret and have a child by her? Or were they perhaps the same person? If only I could find someone who had known him, they might be able to tell me.

Combing the records even further forward I eventually found another marriage certificate for Foster Smith to an Elspeth Fothergill in 1935. If this was the right Foster, he appeared to have been married three times. He was described on the certificate as a widower. So when had Margaret died? More laborious trawling through the Index revealed that Foster had died in 1971 and his death certificate gave me an address in the village of Shiremoor in Northumberland. This made me more hopeful. Northern mining communities are small and close-knit so it was possible that friends and neighbours – maybe even relatives – still lived there. On the spur of the moment I rang the owner of the local post office and asked if there was anyone who might remember Foster. I was immediately given the name of the retired postman – John H. I rang him straight away, and to my delight he told me that Foster had been married to his wife's aunt, Elspeth Fothergill. John was Foster's nephew by marriage.

John was able to give me a good description of Foster, who had not only been an uncle-in-law, but a neighbour. Photographs showed a stocky, rather pugnacious man in shirtsleeves and braces, leaning against the brick wall of his terraced house in Shiremoor, cigarette in hand. He had had a laconic sense

Foster Smith in Shiremoor.

of humour and was notoriously tight with money – 'short arms, long pockets', as they say in the north. Apparently Foster had been seriously injured in an accident at the coal face and despite several operations on his leg he still limped. He had also lost several fingerjoints from his right hand. Hardly surprising that he had become a big union man, though he had to rely on his wife Elspeth to do the paper work. Foster had had little education.

One fact did surprise me. Foster had apparently been a spiritualist. I had known that spiritualism had taken hold in the north-east during the first three decades of the twentieth century. Practitioners were nicknamed 'spooks' and Catherine Cookson often mentioned them in her novels. Foster didn't seem the type to be attracted to the murky world of the medium, seances and mass trances, but when I eventually found out more about his first wife, this seemed less out of character.

John gave me a lot of information, but I was very disappointed when he told me that Foster had rarely said anything about his earlier life. John knew nothing of Elizabeth or Margaret Young, and although he told me that there was a daughter who visited him regularly before he died, John had no idea where she lived. But at least I now knew something about Foster's character – he was becoming a real person. I would have to go back to the St Catherine's Index and get more information about Foster's family. His marriage certificate had given me his age and so I was able to pinpoint which of the four men of that name he actually was. He was not one of the three born in Yorkshire, but had been born in county Durham.

The breakthrough came when I received his birth certificate and discovered that Foster was the child of a young miner called Alexander Smith; his mother was Margaret Foster and he had been born at 3 High Row, Newfield – Jane Davies' family home. Margaret was Jane's older sister, and Foster was her nephew. This explained why Jane might have adopted his

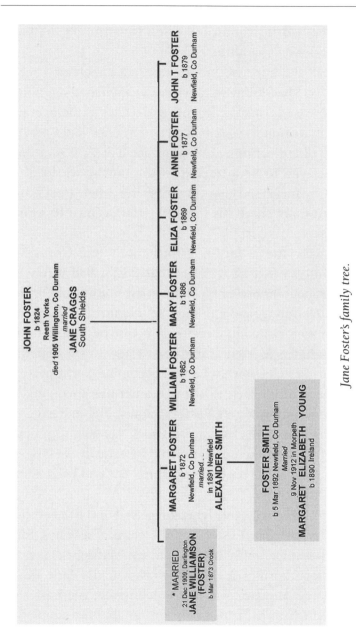

JOHN FOSTER
b 1824
Reeth Yorks
died 1905 Willington, Co Durham
married
JANE CRAGGS
South Shields

MARGARET FOSTER
b 1872
Newfield, Co Durham
married ...
in 1891 Newfield
ALEXANDER SMITH

WILLIAM FOSTER
b 1862
Newfield, Co Durham

MARY FOSTER
b 1866
Newfield, Co Durham

ELIZA FOSTER
b 1869
Newfield, Co Durham

ANNE FOSTER
b 1877
Newfield, Co Durham

JOHN T FOSTER
b 1879
Newfield, Co Durham

* MARRIED
21 Dec 1909, Darlington
**JANE WILLIAMSON
(FOSTER)**
b Mar 1873 Crook

FOSTER SMITH
b 5 Mar 1892 Newfield, Co Durham
Married
9 Nov 1912 in Morpeth
MARGARET ELIZABETH YOUNG
b 1890 Ireland

Jane Foster's family tree.

daughter, and why the baby was named after her. What I still didn't know was why Foster's wife couldn't look after the child herself. I could find no record of her death immediately after the birth of the baby. Had she been ill? And what had happened to the eldest daughter Olive and her mother Elizabeth? There was no mention of them either.

I comforted myself that at least I had solved the puzzle of Alexander's adopted daughter Jane Smith, subsequently Crosby – she was his wife's great-niece, born under his roof and subsequently brought up as his own. But interesting as it all was, none of this information about his wife and family brought me any nearer to knowing who Alexander was and where he had come from. Only his granddaughter – Jane Crosby's daughter – could tell me that, and despite several attempts to contact her it seemed as though she didn't want to talk to me. Once again I was in despair and ready to give up and admit defeat.

7

---·•·---

A PHONE CALL
FROM AMERICA

One evening, as I was preparing supper and watching the television news – Catherine Cookson far from my mind – the telephone rang. A deep voice with a slight Virginian drawl asked if I was Miz Jones? There was some hesitation when I said yes, and then the woman told me that she was Kathy, the daughter of Jane Crosby. She was sorry she'd taken so long to make up her mind to contact me, and explained that her childhood in Scarborough had not been happy and that she was reluctant to go into any of the details. But in the end curiosity had won and she was intrigued to discover why I wanted to know about her grandfather. 'He wasn't my real grandfather, of course,' she said. 'Did you know that?'

Holding my breath and with my fingers crossed, I told Kathy why I needed to know about Alexander Davies, and I also explained that I had never been able to find a birth certificate for him. Kathy immediately became animated. Catherine Cookson's books had been around the house – her mother had apparently owned several of her novels, and

Kathy had watched all the adaptations on satellite channels across the Atlantic. But she was sceptical that there could be any connection, even given the coincidence of the name and the blood disease. Kathy said that she'd brought some of her mother's papers over to America with her when Jane died and that she would look through them and see if there was anything that would help me. By this time she too was intrigued by the mystery of the missing birth certificate. Kathy came over as a warm-hearted person with a big personality.

Two hours later the phone rang again. It was Kathy. Her voice was slightly unsteady with excitement. 'I don't know what this means,' she began, 'but I've got a birth certificate here. It was folded up very small in the bottom of the wallet.' The name on the certificate was Alexander Pate, born in 1879 in Lesmahagow in Scotland. His mother's maiden name was Davies. This, then, was the answer to the riddle. When Alexander wanted to change his name, he had simply adopted his mother's surname. All the other certificates were there too – Alexander's marriage certificate to Jane Foster Williamson, and both their death certificates.

Kathy sent me copies straight away. Alexander's birth certificate was the original, written in decorative Victorian handwriting. It was stained and creased from having been folded and hidden for so long – a hundred and twenty years since his birth in Kirkmuirhill, Lesmahagow. He had been born on 4 December 1879, and his father's name was given as Samuel Pate, an illiterate coal miner who signed his name with a cross. His mother, also illiterate, was Ann Pate, formerly Davies. Scottish birth certificates also give the date of the parents' marriage, which here was given as 2 September 1869, in Lesmahagow. As soon as I could, I went onto the internet to look at the Scots Origins site, and there was the marriage, though it had taken place on the 3rd rather than the 2nd. I was beginning to realize just how unreliable public records could be. In the parish church, Samuel Pate, coal miner, married Sarah Ann Jane Davies, domestic servant and daughter of an Irish labourer called Hugh Davies and his wife Letitia. I ordered a copy, when it finally arrived the certificate gave her surname as Davidson. As both the parties to the marriage were illiterate and signed their names with a cross, none of them would have picked up the error.

I felt quite sure at this point that Alexander Pate and Alexander Davies were the same man. It explained why I had not been able to find a birth certificate for him. And why would Alexander Davies have had another man's birth certificate among his possessions? But I needed to be able to *prove* that they were one individual. I also needed to know why Alexander Davies had changed his identity and taken his mother's maiden name, lied about his father's name and his own age. Most people lie to make themselves younger; Alexander had made himself four years older than he was. Perhaps this was to even the age difference between himself and his wife Jane. He'd admitted to being two years younger when they married, but in reality he was six years younger than her.

Kathy couldn't shed a great deal of light on this. Her step-grandmother had apparently been a very hard woman. If Jane Davies had even suspected that Alexander had deceived her, there would have been hell to pay. Kathy told me that her own mother, Jane Crosby, had always been known as Jenny in the

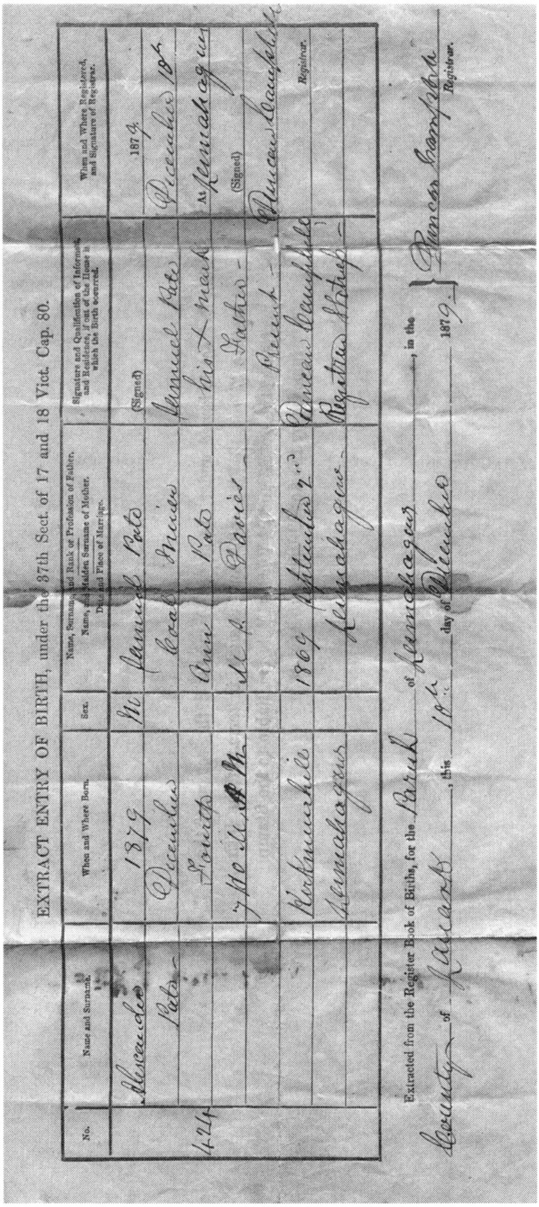

EXTRACT ENTRY OF BIRTH, under the 37th Sect. of 17 and 18 Vict. Cap. 80.

No.	Name and Surname.	When and Where Born.	Sex.	Name, Surname, and Rank or Profession of Father. Name, and Maiden Surname of Mother. Date and Place of Marriage.	Signature and Qualification of Informant, and Residence, if out of the House in which the Birth occurred.	When and Where Registered, and Signature of Registrar.
421	Alexander Pato	1879 December Fourth 7h 0m AM Kirkmuirhill Lesmahagow	M	Samuel Pato Coal Miner Ann Pato MS Davies 1869 September 2nd Lesmahagow	(Signed) Samuel Pato his X mark Father Present Duncan Campbell Registrar Witness	1879 December 18th At Lesmahagow (Signed) Duncan Campbell Registrar.

Extracted from the Register Book of Births, for the Parish of Lesmahagow, in the County of Lanark, this 18th day of December 1879.

Duncan Campbell Registrar.

Alexander's birth certificate.

family to distinguish her from her great-aunt. She had had a very tough upbringing. 'Spare the rod and spoil the child' had been Jane Davies' favourite maxim. Having had no children of her own, she wasn't inclined to dote on her adopted daughter. There had been little love in the house, though Jenny had been very fond of her adoptive father Alexander, and had looked after him devotedly after his wife died. He'd suffered very badly from HHT, Kathy said. Her mother had told her that at times she would have to put a bucket in front of him and watch him bleed pints into it, until she feared he would bleed to death. He had begun to bleed not only from the nose but also from the stomach; the doctors at first diagnosed a bleeding gastric ulcer. Little was known about HHT in those days – he was very lucky to have it diagnosed at all. More recent research has shown how it spreads down into the stomach, causing haemorrhages known as hae-metemesis. Catherine Cookson herself suffered from this and actually bought the laser machine needed to cauterize the rogue blood vessels for Newcastle's Royal Victoria Infirmary. No such treatment was available for Alexander Davies in 1948 and it was a haemorrhage from the stomach that was the major cause of his death.

He left the house and its contents to his adopted daughter, who had, in the months before his death, married George Crosby. Apparently he had been a very strict father to her. Kathy said that her mother had been very much in love with someone else and wanted to marry him, but Alexander had forbidden it because he said the man was a scoundrel. So Jenny had refused him, but regretted afterwards being so sensible. There were lots of other things I wanted to know, and over the weeks that followed, in emails and telephone calls, Kathy revealed to me more fragments of her family history. How had Alexander afforded a house in Scarborough, I asked? He had apparently been a bookie – and his gambling was notorious. He would bet thousands (and this was the 1930s and 1940s) on a horse, sometimes losing, sometimes winning, and then he would splash out on things. His wife was good at squirrelling money away when she could get her hands on it. Alexander was unreliable with money. Kathy described him to me as a handsome, dapper man, always beautifully dressed and groomed. People had told her that he looked like John le Mesurier. He was charming and well-spoken, but also a bit of a rogue. This description certainly fitted with that of the Alexander Davies that Kate had known – someone who had taken her to the races, who spoke beautifully, was charming but unreliable and dressed well. There was also the common element of theatricality – he had reminded Kate's sister Mary of the Silver King in the music hall; in the 1940s he reminded people of John le Mesurier. Was this the same man? I had my fingers crossed.

Kathy also began to tell me more about her own childhood. Like Catherine Cookson's it had been full of secrets. She had not been told the truth of her family history at all. Her father's family, the Crosbys, were local to Scarborough, so she knew that side of her parentage, but her mother's was shrouded in mystery. Both Alexander and Jane Davies were dead by the time Kathy was born, though their possessions and photographs crowded the house as she was growing up. Her mother Jenny would rarely talk about her own relatives and often suffered very badly from depression. But Kathy found out, very gradually, about what she called her 'dark family'. Since her birth, Jenny had had little contact with her real father, Foster Smith. Kathy eventually discovered that there was an older sister – an aunt called Olive – and there were cousins. But no one seemed to know what had happened to Foster Smith's wife Margaret, Kathy's real grandmother. No one would talk about her.

Kathy's mother Jenny became increasingly strict and reclusive. Eventually Kathy couldn't stand it any longer and at fifteen she left home abruptly and took the bus back to the north-east, to try to find the relatives she had never known. When she arrived on her aunt Olive's doorstep it caused consternation. Olive had married a miner in 1931 and had four children, two girls and two boys, who were now almost grown up. She took Kathy in and tried to answer her questions. Foster Smith lived nearby with his second wife Elspeth, and Kathy was taken to visit her real grandfather for the first time. But mystery still surrounded her grandmother. It appeared that Margaret/Elizabeth might be the same person, known by two different names. There were also conflicting stories about her health. Kathy was told that after Olive's birth, Foster's wife had been very ill. No one seemed to be exactly sure about the nature of her illness. Kathy's mother Jenny said that she had been mentally ill; Olive told her children that it was tuberculosis. Whatever it was, Margaret/Elizabeth had been a permanent invalid. After Olive's birth in 1913, Foster's family moved in with Jane and Alexander Davies. When Foster's wife was too ill to look after the child, Jane Davies had brought her up. The family told Kathy that when Jenny was born, her grandmother had again been ill and had gone

Jenny in middle age.

into a sanatorium. She had eventually died – of tuberculosis, they believed. Margaret's eldest daughter Olive – old enough to look after herself by then – stayed with her father Foster Smith but Jenny was taken away to be brought up by her maternal aunt, Jane Davies.

Foster Smith's wife's name-changing still puzzled me. But after a great deal of searching, I eventually found a birth certificate for a Margaret Lizzie Young, who was born in the right area at the right time and had the same father's name as the man on their marriage certificate. She was born in Morpeth, and I knew that the family had been living in Ashington, only a few miles away, when she married. She appeared to have styled herself variously as Elizabeth or Margaret on any number of official forms. And what was the truth about her health? Had she suffered from tuberculosis, as Olive had insisted, or from the mental health problems Kathy's mother Jenny had talked about? For whatever reason, Margaret, it seemed, had been unable to look after either of her daughters. How tragic too for Foster Smith, who was married to a woman he rarely saw in the twenty years that she was alive after their marriage.

I now knew a lot more of the history of Alexander's adopted family, but very little about the enigmatic man with the dual identity who was at the heart of the story. If I wanted to prove beyond reasonable doubt that these two men were the same person, and that this was Catherine Cookson's father, I would have to trace Alexander Pate forwards from his birthplace to see if his history coincided with that of Alexander Davies. And there was still nothing to suggest that he had been anywhere near Lamesley in 1904. I would need to go to Scotland, to Lesmahagow, to find out more.

8

---•◆•---

LESMAHAGOW

Lesmahagow is in Lanarkshire, just off the main M74 motorway, about twenty-five miles south of Glasgow. Like many communities in county Durham and parts of Northumberland, it was once part of a string of mining villages that followed the rich coal seams underground. Most of them have gone now and the rolling Scottish landscape is once more green and lush, given over to farming again. Villages such as Coalburn, Douglas Water, Kirkmuirhill and Lesmahagow, where the Pate family lived during the second half of the nineteenth century, seem somehow to have lost the purpose for which they were created. The rows of miners' houses have been pulled down over the years and only the older houses are left on either side of the main road – buildings that pre-date the Industrial Revolution.

Scottish records are, however, much more easily accessed than those in England. Not only are all the registrations of birth, marriage and death available to members of the public on the internet (for a small charge), local registrars will open their books to you (again for a small charge) so that you can work through the records and note down every relevant detail,

Lesmahagow as it is today, the church in which Alexander's parents were married and the graveyard where members of his family are buried.

including witnesses to marriages, and the addresses. Without having to send off for expensive certificates, you can see immediately which children were born to which parents; which survived and which died in infancy. With a clan as large as the Pates, this was very important. In addition, the library in Lanark held all the county records.

I was very quickly given the Census records back to the 1850s, for all the villages where I knew the Pate family had lived, as well as having access to older records. With these I could trace the history of the Pate family back to a couple called John and Mary, who in 1779 had a child called Alexander. From this first recorded Alexander I could follow the generations forward until I found the one I was looking for. Samuel Pate, my Alexander's father, was a coal miner, one of a large family of Pates who mostly worked down the mines, though a few still worked the land. The same names recurred through the generations: Samuel, Alexander, Thomas or William. The girls were called Jeanie, Elizabeth, Agnes, Isabella and Mary. This created confusion: there was a tradition of naming the first son after the father and the next two after their grandfathers; and the girls after their mothers and grandmothers. So Alexander's eldest brother was called Samuel after his father, and his older brother after his mother's Irish father – Hugh. Alexander was named for his great-grandfather. His older sister was called Letty after their maternal grandmother Letitia.

The Pate family seemed to have been prolific. There were at least eight groups of them living in the area, and Alexander himself was one of eleven children. In the Census for 1891, Samuel Pate and his wife Ann Davies were living at 5 Thornton Place in Lesmahagow, a dwelling that had only two rooms. The eldest son Samuel had left home and was living in lodgings, but the rest of the children were still at home. The oldest girl Elizabeth was eighteen and working as a domestic servant. Hugh, at fifteen, was already employed as an engine keeper in the mines and – more shocking – his thirteen-year-old sister Letty was doing the same job. Alexander, at only eleven was listed as being at school along with his younger brother and sisters, Mary, nine, Grace, seven, and William, five. The babies of the family were Marion aged three and Jeanie, only ten months. I found myself wondering where they all slept and how their mother managed when wet weather kept the children inside, but such privation was common then. All their relations lived nearby in similar conditions. Ann Pate's father Hugh Davies and his wife also lived in the village with assorted children and grandchildren lodged with them.

In the cemetery behind the beautiful Presbyterian church where Alexander's parents were married, I found all the Pate graves. This was unusual as very poor families could rarely afford gravestones. Even if they were not buried in an unmarked pauper's grave, a wooden cross was often all that could be afforded, and this soon rotted away, leaving no record of the person beneath the ground. This is one of the difficulties of tracing 'working-class' ancestors. The Pates, however, seem to have found the money to erect family memorials: along the back wall of the churchyard, among the oldest tombstones, were a series of Pate graves, including the oldest of their ancestors, John Pate and Mary Portress. Looking at their carved headstones, it seemed that the Pates had not always been as poor as Alexander's family.

Samuel Pate and his father-in-law not only laboured below and above ground, they seem to have bred horses in a small way. This was common in mining communities in the northeast too. Horses were the motor cars and commercial engines of the day and vast numbers of them were needed for industrial and private use. The mines used horses to pull the coal tubs underground and to turn the wheels at the pit head, as well as for carting coal and slag. Many miners, if they could get the money together to buy a mare in foal, would tether the horse on common ground, or on the roadside verges, and rear the foals to sell when they were mature enough. Presumably Samuel, with his family farming connections, or perhaps Hugh with his links to the Irish drovers of Donegal, had somehow acquired the first mare to begin the trade. From then on it was a profitable sideline that would put shoes on the children's feet and bread in their mouths.

The poverty was unimaginable and quite comparable to the straitened circumstances of Kate Fawcett's childhood in South Shields, and later to her daughter Catherine's. I found myself wondering at what point Alexander had looked at the slag heaps and the rows of neglected houses, the sky above them darkened by chimney smoke and coal dust, and vowed to get out of it. Like his daughter, he seemed to be driven by the desire to have a better life than the one he had been born to, but his urge certainly wasn't in the family tradition. The Pates had remained settled in Lesmahagow since the seventeenth

Colliery houses in Douglas Water where Alexander spent part of his childhood.

105

century. Only one member of the family seems to have shown a little more entrepreneurial spirit, two hundred years earlier, by going off to America and publishing his memoirs. Alexander was apparently different from his brothers and sisters, a restless spirit, a dreamer and a story-teller. He soaked up the little education he was given enthusiastically, before the necessities of life in a coal-mining community forced him into unskilled manual labour at the age of thirteen. Later in life he gave the impression of someone cultured and 'book-learned'; he was also clever with his pencil, dashing off little drawings on the backs of envelopes.

After 1895, although other family members turned up regularly in the local records, I found no other mention of the young Alexander: he simply disappeared. Had he left the mines to get a job somewhere else? Had he perhaps gone to sea? Once again, after a run of luck, I had come up against a brick wall.

9

---•••---

THE NEWCASTLE BREWERS

It was only a hunch, but I reasoned that if this man was the right Alexander, he might well have migrated to the northeast straight from Lesmahagow at any time after 1895. Perhaps, given the fact that he had 'marine engineer' entered on his death certificate, he had joined the merchant navy and come to Newcastle as a sailor. So I went down to London to look in the records of the Registrar General of Shipping and Seamen held in the Public Record Office and the National Maritime Museum at Greenwich. Each ship registered under the Merchant Shipping Act of 1854 had to keep crew lists and official logs, which were then stored. It was also obligatory for the master of the ship to enter into an agreement with every member of his crew and these agreements were also preserved. Unfortunately, the great bulk of paperwork meant that it was impractical for it all to be kept, so, prior to 1921, only a random 10 per cent sample for each year is actually retained in the archives. The National Maritime Museum has all the rest, but only for one year in five. Finding Alexander Davies as an ordinary seaman, even if I had known the names of his ships, proved an impossible task. For an officer, things are rather different. Masters, Mates and Engineers all had to be properly certificated and all these records are preserved. If Alexander really had been a marine engineer, as he claimed, he would have had to obtain certificates of competency at various levels; even the most junior were required to have a certificate. So I trawled through all the books, and although I found the William Fawcett who had witnessed his marriage to Jane, Alexander's name did not come up at all, even as an apprentice. It seemed his claim was false.

However he had come to the north-east, he was certainly there by the time of his marriage to Jane in 1909, so I began to look through the records between 1895 and 1908 for any mention of the name Pate in Durham and Northumberland. Sure enough there was a small group of Pates, living in the Newcastle area and working in the mines north of the Tyne. Then, unexpectedly, I came across an entry for the marriage of an Alexander Pate in 1901. This wasn't necessarily significant – my Alexander had at least three cousins and an uncle with the same name! I sent away for the certificate and could hardly wait the four days it took to arrive. Registrars are busy people, and the explosion of interest in people tracing their own genealogy has added considerably to their workload over the last two or three years.

When the certificate arrived it was indeed the man I was looking for. Alexander Pate, aged twenty-three, had married a twenty-year-old girl called Henrietta Waggott in Newcastle Register Office. His occupation was given as stonemason, and he was living at 28 Strickland Street, Newcastle. His father Samuel Pate was described as a horsedealer. Everywhere else Samuel is listed under his primary occupation of coal miner, but not here. Did Alexander want to seem rather better than he was? There were also distinct reminders here of Alexander Davies' marriage certificate to Jane – he too had described his father as a horsedealer. Henrietta's father was named as John Waggott and the marriage had been witnessed by the local doctor Albert E. May and Henrietta's sister, Jenny. The name Waggott rang bells in my mind, but I couldn't remember why. During the search I had made lists of so many people, I'd reached the stage where almost every name I read seemed familiar. But there were nagging echoes as I set out to find out as much as I could about the Waggott family.

If Alexander was really Catherine's father then Aunt Mary's gossip had not been far from the truth. He wasn't the son of a brewer, but had been married to the daughter of a brewing family. Henrietta's grandparents were brewers of a small but well-known brand of Newcastle ale. At the time of the marriage they were living in retirement in the Hexham area, in a beautiful, detached Victorian house standing in its own gardens. If Alexander had thought to better himself after leaving Lesmahagow, such a marriage might have been very timely, but the Waggotts were no longer rich. The brewery income had declined in recent years and it wasn't as profitable as it had once been, but there was still the feeling of respectable middle-class comfort. Their son John had become a postman – not the rather humdrum occupation it is today, but a very responsible job with all the status of a civil service career, though still commanding only a modest salary. John Waggott and his family lived in a terraced Victorian house. Apart from his daughter Henrietta, there were three other daughters and a son. Family photographs show a typical

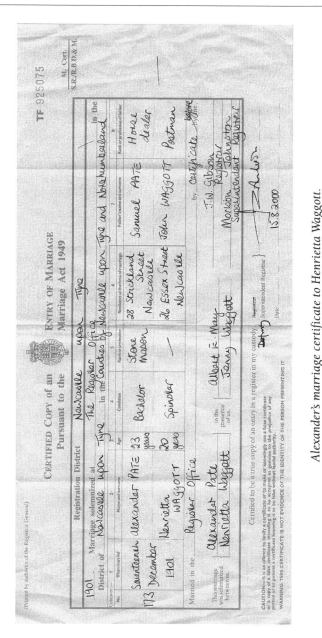

Alexander's marriage certificate to Henrietta Waggott.

The Waggott family around 1899 – Henrietta standing in the centre.

nineteenth-century household and have an air of stifling respectability: the dark coloured satin and bombazine dresses trimmed with floss and braid; the stiff hairstyles and composed faces. John Waggott is the archetypal Victorian father, with walrus moustache and a broad expanse of waistcoat decorated with a watchchain. Henrietta, standing at the back between her parents, looks slim and pretty, but has a rather sharp look in her eyes and a very determined chin.

My next task was to find out if Alexander and Henrietta had had any children, and to my amazement found the record of the birth of a son straight away. When the certificate arrived it was obvious that Alexander, far from making himself an ambitious marriage, had not gone willingly to the altar at all. The marriage had taken place on 17 December 1901 and

Henrietta's child, also called Alexander, was born three weeks later on 2 January 1982. Nor was she living in comfort. The address given was a lodging house in Carville Road, Byker. I wondered what kind of man could make a respectable girl like Henrietta pregnant and then prevaricate over marriage until she was almost nine months gone. She must have been utterly distraught. Had he loved her at all? And how had the family persuaded such a reluctant man to make an honest woman of her in the end? The significance of the local doctor's signature on the marriage certificate seemed clear – doctors wielded considerable social clout in those days. Later I found that the doctor was also Henrietta's maternal uncle, which would have increased his influence considerably.

Following the records forward again I discovered that in February 1904, at yet another address, a baby girl called Henrietta was born. This time Alexander is described as a labourer at the Elswick steelworks – a step down from stone-masonry. When I was finally able to talk to his grandchildren, they told a tale of domestic discord. Alexander had been 'a good-looking nowt', a charmer, a ladies man, a gambler and a cheat. His spectacular good looks had become a family legend. Henrietta Waggott's sisters told his children that he had resembled Rudolph Valentino in his most famous role as the Sheikh of Araby. One of his granddaughters preserved a newspaper cutting of the film star, the nearest she could get to a photograph of her missing grandfather. When he wasn't working Alexander Pate was given to natty dressing – wearing expensive clothes and very proud of the silver-topped cane he took with him whenever he went out. He didn't hold down any kind of job for long – his real life was lived on the racecourses of the north-east. In an art gallery in Gateshead there is a painting of Blaydon racecourse in 1903 that portrays the kind of company that Alexander kept: characters such as Tommy Diddle the Tipster, Bob the Wrong'un, George the Plunger, Billy Sup-up, Scrapper Reed, and women such as the Belle of Wylam, Nanny the Maser or Mussell Nell.

In this culture of nicknames and aliases, Alexander himself used other names to escape creditors, and was increasingly leading a double life. It was his gambling debts that caused the most misery in the household – Henrietta never knew when the bailiffs were going to arrive to take away her furniture and there was often no money to pay the rent or to buy food. Three times her home was emptied to the bare boards. Her parents helped out when they could, but Alexander's debts were beyond their limited means and they had other children to educate and launch into the world. Henrietta was told that, having transgressed the moral code by becoming pregnant before marriage, she had made her bed and must lie on it. They had done their best by ensuring that Alexander marry her rather than leave her to the shame and disgrace of being an unmarried mother.

The situation led to great bitterness, as romantic love was eroded by hardship and betrayal. Henrietta had a sharp tongue in her head and made Alexander well aware of what she thought of him. There were long periods when he left her, reappearing occasionally to put money on the table. Most of this money came from gambling – mainly on horses. The 1901 Census, when it eventually became available in 2001, answered a lot of questions. It revealed that Alexander had come to Newcastle after the death of his father and brought

Henrietta shortly before her marriage.

his mother and his four younger siblings with him. His sister Grace worked as a domestic servant, an occupation soon taken up by the two other girls, Marion and Jeanie. During the repeated separations from his wife he may well have gone back to live with his mother. Later on he lodged with his younger sister Jeanie, who never married. The two siblings, though twelve years apart in age, were very close and remained in contact until Alexander died, providing an open channel of communication between one life and another. There was also an eight-year-old brother James, who eventually married a girl who came from Gateshead – not far from where Kate worked. Descendants of this branch of the Pate family still live in the area.

After February 1904 there were no more records of any children born to the couple, and I assumed for a while that they had separated for good. This was the period, after all, when – if he *was* Catherine's father – he was seeing Kate in Lamesley. But then suddenly, in October 1908, there was the birth of another girl, Isabella, and this time Alexander – living at yet another address – is listed as being a hand driller in the shipyard. When I finally met them, his grandchildren told me that Henrietta had taken him back for just one last chance, but that hadn't even lasted until the birth of the child. There had been another row – over money, or another woman, no one was sure – and, even though she realized that she was pregnant again, Henrietta threw him out, telling him that she never, ever, wanted to see him or hear from him again.

This final ultimatum was a proviso that her parents had insisted on. They were willing to take her back into their home with her children, to rescue her from destitution, provided that she cut herself off completely from her good-for-nothing husband. Henrietta swallowed her pride and went back to live with her parents. From then on she had to find the means to earn the money for her children's support. The Waggotts declared that they weren't wealthy enough to feed and clothe four extra family members. Their help seems to have been grudgingly given. Like Kate Fawcett, on the other side of the Tyne, Henrietta was reduced to a life of domestic drudgery, having to find paid work in order to feed her children.

According to Alexander's grandchildren, he stayed away for almost a year, until one evening he came to the back-door and told one of the children that he would like to see his wife. They talked in the washhouse in the yard – a conversation overheard by Henrietta's youngest sister Isabella. He pleaded with her to give him a divorce so that he would be free to marry again, but Henrietta refused. It would be a public humiliation for her, she said, to have her name in the papers like that. It wasn't even to be considered. Alexander took his hat and walked out into the night and at that point, as far as the public record was concerned, Alexander Pate ceased to exist.

10

ABANDONED WOMEN

It is ironic that, while Henrietta Pate was going through the traumas of the abandoned wife on the northern side of the Tyne, Kate Fawcett was having a similar struggle to support her illegitimate daughter, living with her parents in South Shields, only a couple of miles away across the water. The physical drudgery left Kate so exhausted that she would fall asleep in her chair at the table while eating her supper. She suffered from depression, which she drowned in drink: beer and whisky were her favourites. Catherine remembered, and blamed her mother all her life, for the trips she had to make as a child to the liquor store, where she would either fill a big stoneware flagon called a 'grey hen' or purchase a little flat bottle of golden liquid wrapped up in brown paper. Catherine was sent because her mother was ashamed of being seen there. The pawn shop was another regular destination. Nicknamed the 'in and out', if you were really poor you pawned the blankets off the bed in the morning to get the bread knife and the frying pan out for breakfast and then made the reverse trip in the evening. Coats and suits worn only for best were a staple: they would only be taken out when needed. But Kate rarely had anything so respectable to pawn. Catherine said that she was shamed by the shabby articles the pawnbroker took out of the parcel and fingered in front of everyone in the shop, offering only a pitiful amount of money for them.

Catherine regularly picked coal up off the street, one of a flock of poor children who followed the coal wagons from the wharves. Sometimes she went to the tip with her Uncle Jack to pick coal from the waste. At other times she combed the banks of the river at low tide for driftwood for the fire. Twice she nearly drowned. Those were the experiences that stayed with Catherine throughout her life, like grit in the flesh of an oyster, and their irritation was the stimulus for her novels.

Kate had been bred to this kind of hardship – she had known little else since she was born and she had a phenomenally strong constitution. Her ability to work ten hours a day, seven days a week, was legendary and it made her a much-sought after employee for the people whose houses she cleaned. Henrietta Waggott had been born to a different kind of life. She was physically small-boned and thin, without Kate's strong frame. Her childhood had been protected by her parents' financial security and she had never wanted for anything. She had never been out to work and the most she had ever had to do at home were light domestic tasks. Suddenly, when her husband left, she was exposed to a very different life style. Although her parents had taken her in again, with her three children, they made it clear that they weren't going to offer her anything more than a roof over her head. It was as though they were determined to punish her for her mistaken choice of husband. After years of turmoil and anxiety, Henrietta now faced not only the emotional misery of a failed marriage but, having refused Alexander a divorce, she had to endure a permanent, lonely separation. She was in limbo – there was no prospect of a second chance for her, unless her husband died. Henrietta was still only twenty-seven. Not only did she have to look after her ageing parents, but she had to take in washing and go out cleaning for others in order to support her children. She was also employed by many poor women, unable to afford proper medical attention, to deliver their children, and by other families to lay out the dead. Where Kate had taken to drink to ease her misery, Henrietta took refuge in religion and became increasingly devout.

By the time the First World War broke out, the Pate children were growing up fast. Young Alexander was nearly thirteen – tall, dark-haired and as handsome as his father. Henrietta viewed his phenomenal good looks with suspicion, but the younger Alexander could not have been more unlike his father. He was a kind and dutiful boy, who spent a great deal of time looking after his mother and his younger sisters. Like his father he was academically bright and Henrietta was determined that he should have his chances and not have his life blighted by financial constraints. She was delighted, when at the age of fourteen, he was taken on as a junior clerk by a big shipping company on the Tyne.

The girls, too, particularly the young Henrietta – now known as Letty to distinguish her from her mother – were growing into attractive young women. Henrietta was determined that they shouldn't make the same mistake as she had

Henrietta and her children in 1910.

done, and her bitterness was caustic. They were told over and over again – 'Don't marry a good-looking nowt!' No marriage was better than a bad marriage. Henrietta had destroyed every photograph of Alexander, every reminder of him. As far as she was concerned, he was dead. But she still kept in touch with Jeanie, his younger sister in domestic service in Newcastle. Or perhaps it was Jeanie who kept in touch with her nephew and nieces. Through Jeanie, Alexander was able to get news of his children and his wife. When eventually grandchildren were born, mysterious, sometimes extravagant presents arrived, delivered by their great-aunt.

I wasn't able to find out where Alexander Pate, now living as Alexander Davies, spent the war years between 1914 and 1918, or whether he served in any of the armed forces. His friend and nephew by marriage, Foster Smith, went into the merchant navy below decks – as a miner I suppose he was ideally suited to endure the claustrophobic conditions. So perhaps it's possible that Alexander also served in the merchant marine during the war, and this may have explained his son-in-law's description of him as a 'marine engineer, retired' on his death certificate. But equally it was possible that Alexander's occasional work in the shipyards as a driller and labourer was embroidered in later life into something much more substantial and respectable. Whatever he did, Alexander reappeared after the war, living with Foster Smith and working in the coal mines, the very life he had tried to leave behind in Lesmahagow.

On the other side of the Tyne, Kate's prospects actually improved during the war. Her half-brother Jack was killed, and though she mourned him there was also a sense of relief

The Newcastle Brewers (Pate Family).

that the sexual persecution he had subjected her to had come to an end. There was now only Kate, Catherine and her step-grandfather John McMullen in the house, which made it easier to take in lodgers for a living. In 1920, while Alexander Davies was living at Witton le Wear, Catherine left school and went out to work, at first in service and then at Harton workhouse laundry as a checker. One of the lodgers, a merchant seaman called David McDermott, asked Kate to marry him and she quickly agreed, achieving respectability and status for the first time in her life. He was also well paid, putting an end to Kate's life of drudgery.

But there was no such alleviation in store for Henrietta. The hard physical work ruined her constitution and she became prematurely old. She was increasingly protective towards her children, leaning particularly on her eldest son Alexander. He was doing well as a commercial clerk in the shipping office. The firm thought highly of his work and his character and he was quickly promoted through the ranks, with corresponding increases in pay. His future seemed secure when he met a young girl called Elsie Moul. She was the daughter of a fireman in the steelworks and lived quietly at home. Women didn't automatically have jobs in those days: if finances permitted, most girls stayed at home and helped their mothers until they got married. But things didn't run smoothly with the romance. Elsie was religious and very respectable and wanted, not surprisingly in view of his family history, to make sure of Alexander's affections. Alexander was hardly in a position to take a wife, as he was still supporting his mother, who was not the easiest of women to please. Henrietta did not like the idea of Alexander marrying Elsie, but in February

1923 the twenty-one-year-old married Elsie in Newcastle Register Office in the presence of her brother and her sister. After the ceremony Elsie hung her wedding ring on a chain around her neck and they went home separately.

Elsie, who is still alive, aged almost a hundred, had never told any of her children about this early wedding ceremony and can give no explanation for it. Whether it was in the nature of an engagement, or to thwart Henrietta, no one seems to know. Elsie's parents must have consented, because – at only nineteen – she would have needed their permission. It wasn't until 1926, three years later, that Elsie and Alexander were married again in St James' Church, Benwell, and went home together as man and wife. A year later their eldest son Reginald Alexander was born.

Meanwhile Henrietta's health continued to decline. Before her grandson was born, although still only in her early forties, she had suffered a series of strokes and in 1928, at the ridiculously young age of forty-seven, she died suddenly at home from heart failure following another massive stroke. The family were distraught. Although Alexander had married, Letty was still single and the youngest daughter Isabella was only twenty – still a minor in those days. Letty was living with her Aunt Jenny in Newark, working in the shop in return for her keep. Isabella had a good job with a printer but wasn't earning enough to keep a roof over her head, so she went to live with her Aunt Isabella in Newcastle.

Henrietta died on 30 December 1928, shortly after the twenty-seventh anniversary of her unfortunate marriage. At the funeral, on a grey January day, Henrietta's family paid tribute to her courage and mourned the tragedy of her life. It

The Waggott family grave after Henrietta's funeral.

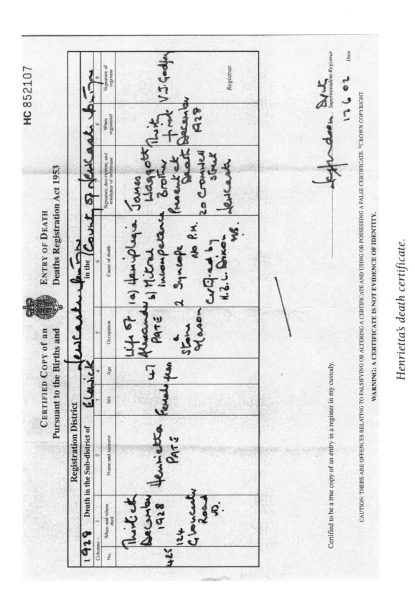

Henrietta's death certificate.

was a sombre occasion. After the service, as her son walked out of the church behind the coffin, Alexander saw a tall, thin man in dark clothing standing unobtrusively at the back. Although he hadn't seen him since he was a small child, Alexander instinctively recognized his father. Informed of his wife's death by his sister Jeanie, Alexander Davies had come back to pay his last respects.

On Alexander and Elsie's marriage certificate, Alexander Pate senior is described as being 'deceased' but – as on Catherine Cookson's marriage certificate – this seems to have been a convenient fiction, since Henrietta's brother, in registering her death, describes her as being the wife, not the widow, of Alexander Pate. The family were obviously aware of his continuing existence, presumably through Jeanie, even if they didn't know of his new identity.

Amazingly, even though Henrietta's sisters and brother all recognized her errant husband at the funeral, neither Letty nor Isabella were told that their father was in the church until afterwards. Apparently the young Alexander had an emotional reunion with his father and they talked for a long time. They promised to keep in direct contact with each other in future, though out of respect for the circumstances and Alexander's new identity it was to be kept secret. When this story was told to me, it was the first time that the two halves of Alexander's life had come together. Alexander Pate and Alexander Davies were the same man.

11

———— ·•· ————

THE PATE FAMILY

In order to prove conclusively that Alexander Pate and Alexander Davies were the same man, I needed more than just circumstantial evidence (although that was now overwhelming) or family stories. The details of his appearance and character, the fact that one man died with the other's birth certificate in his possession, would be persuasive on their own, but I needed something more. If they were one and the same, then Alexander Pate had to have suffered from the same blood disease as Alexander Davies and some of the children of his first marriage would also have inherited the rare hereditary haemorrhagic telangiectasis that he had passed on to Catherine. The likelihood of transmission of this disease from parent to child is rather more than 50 per cent. I would have to trace Alexander's children, or their descendants, in order to find out. It was probable, too, that they might know a great deal more about his life story than I did – details that might help me to prove the link to Catherine Cookson.

I began to trace the Pate children forwards through the twentieth century. Alexander, I knew, had married Elsie Moul. I was still mystified by the fact that they had been married twice – once in 1923 and again in 1926. Alexander's eldest sister Letty had married Arthur Robinson, a storeman in Newark, in 1932, while Isabella, the youngest, married a motor mechanic called Thomas McFarlane in 1935 in Newcastle. Painstakingly I went through the births, year by year, starting with the dates of their marriages. Fortunately the way births are recorded in the indexes was changed just before the First World War, and as well as the father's surname the mother's maiden name is also given, so it's much easier to find the birth of a child to a particular set of parents. Alexander and Elsie had three children. The certificates showed me that Reginald Alexander and Kenneth were both born in Blyth in 1927 and 1929, and by this time their father was described as a shipping broker. A daughter, Muriel, was born later after the family moved to Scotland. I was later told that Alexander had been given backing by the company who employed him to set up a ship brokerage and coal merchant's business in Wick – almost as far north as you can go. Letty, who made a relatively late marriage, and whose health was always fragile, had only one daughter, Ann. Isabella – affectionately known in the family as Belsie – was still living in Newcastle when her two daughters Sheila and June were born. She was the only child who appeared to have stayed in the north-east and I hoped that I would be able to find her.

Needing more recent addresses, I began to look through the register of deaths. I still hoped that at least one of the children would still be alive: Isabella wasn't born until 1908, so would be in her nineties, but many people live to that age now. Beginning with the last mention of each one on record, I combed the St Catherine's Index for Pate deaths. Surprisingly

Half-Sisters? Isabella Pate (left) and Catherine Cookson in old age.

quickly I found the death of an Alexander Pate in Bournemouth in 1954. When the certificate arrived, I was saddened to find that this was the young Alexander. He had died at the early age of fifty-two from a massive coronary, surviving his father by only seven years. The death was registered by his son Reginald Alexander – still living at their home address, which was now given as Hertfordshire. Later I found that Alexander had moved from Scotland to the south of England only a couple of years before his death. Although only in his forties, he – like his mother – had begun to suffer from angina. Worried by her husband's ill-health Elsie wanted to be nearer to her family who had all migrated south. Alexander was willing to take a retrograde step, sell his own business and go back to working for someone else in order to improve his health and please his wife. He was a conscientious man who regularly overworked. The stress associated with the move, combined with the heart disease that was in his genes, all contributed to the heart attack that came when he and Elsie were having a holiday in Bournemouth, visiting her relatives. Heart disease was a family hazard. His younger son Kenneth died in 1994 from the same cause, but both Muriel and Reginald were still alive in 1999. In order to get recent addresses, I tracked their marriages and their children's births, thankful that Pate was not a common name in England.

Alexander junior's sister Letty, I discovered, had also died young – but not from heart disease. She died of a haemorrhage associated with haemorrhagic telangiectasis. This was my first real proof that Alexander Pate and Alexander Davies were the same man.

My hopes were now pinned on Isabella, but sadly I discovered that she too had died in 1990. Her daughter Sheila had registered the death and there was an address in Whitley Bay on the form as well as Sheila's married name. The family were obviously still living in the north-east. I searched the electoral rolls and telephone directories for all the areas where I knew the Pate family had lived and found both Reginald and Sheila. Neither Muriel nor Ann appeared, but I didn't yet know their married names. Their details and those of Sheila's sister June would come later. In the meantime I wrote tactful letters to both Reginald and Sheila, simply saying that I was tracing the history of the Pate family and had information on their grandfather, Alexander, which they might like to have.

On impulse, I dialled Sheila's number. I don't know why, I hate cold calling and would be very suspicious of a stranger wanting details of my family history over the phone. Looking back, I think I was so excited by the thought of being able to talk to a living member of Alexander's family after tracking him on paper for so long, I simply couldn't stand the suspense of having to wait for a reply to a letter! A warm, lively voice with a north-eastern accent answered the phone and I explained, in a halting, awkward kind of way, who I was, that I was tracing the history of her family and was very interested in anything she might have been told about her grandfather Alexander Pate. I was particularly interested to know whether there was any history of HHT in her family. 'This wouldn't be anything to do with Catherine Cookson, would it?' Sheila asked crisply. Cautiously I asked why. 'Well,' she said, 'We've always suspected that we might be related.'

I arranged to go over to Whitley Bay to meet Sheila and her sister June the following week. When the day came, the appointment coincided with a national petrol strike and I almost cancelled. Then I decided that I probably had enough petrol in the tank to get there and back, if I was careful, so I took the risk. When I arrived at Sheila's house and rang the bell, her sister June answered the door. I was made very welcome and offered coffee and a lavish display of biscuits and cakes. Sheila was upstairs getting changed after walking the dog. I turned, hearing footsteps, and was absolutely amazed to see a Catherine Cookson lookalike coming down the stairs – the face, the eyes, the auburn hair and the lively, outgoing manner were uncannily like a younger version of Catherine. Both she and her sister June were amazingly alike and I could see why the family might have suspected a connection.

As we talked, it was obvious that their suspicious were based on more substantial evidence than mere familial resemblance. Several members of the family shared the same inherited disease as Catherine. Their grandfather had been called Alexander, the same as her father. He was also a womanizer and a gambler. Then there were the long separations from his wife, the secret life and the other women that Henrietta had been aware of. Sheila said that she would not be surprised to find that he had fathered other children in the north-east. Henrietta Waggott's sister Isabella, known affectionately as Aunty Belle, had lived with Sheila and June's mother until she died and consequently they knew far more about their history than other family members.

June and Sheila – Isabella Pate's daughters.

Sheila and June showed me the family photograph album: Henrietta as she was before she married Alexander; an older Henrietta with her three abandoned children; then photographs of the children as adults. The eldest daughter, Letty, had suffered most from HHT. She had been sent to live with Waggott relatives in Newark, who had offered to pay for her medical treatment. She had met her husband and subsequently settled there. Letty's photographs were striking. If you put them side by side with Catherine Cookson at about the same age it was impossible to tell which was which. That they were half-sisters seemed indisputable, though I still had to prove it.

I asked Sheila and June if they knew what had happened to their grandfather after he left in 1907, but all they had been told was that, after refusing him a divorce, Henrietta had never seen him again. They had often wondered where he had gone, and Sheila had in fact just enrolled in night classes to trace her genealogy. I was able to put Alexander Pate's birth certificate and his marriage certificate on the table and then show them the certificates bearing the name Alexander Davies. The signature is the same on both the originals. It became obvious now that the reason Alexander had changed his name and his age and family details was in order to commit bigamy. But he seems to have used his mother's maiden name earlier, to avoid his creditors and to facilitate his romantic adventures, and from 1909 he used it exclusively. The falsification of his date of birth was, presumably, to make the age difference between himself and his second wife less obvious, and he must have known it would make the fraud less easy to trace. The change of his father's name from Samuel

Letty and Catherine at very similar ages.

to Alexander was a stroke of inspiration. It was at this point that I discovered that one of my seven original Alexanders – the Alexander Davis, son of Alexander, dock labourer in Glasgow – was actually a second cousin. Knowing that he had a second cousin with the same name, it must have been easy for Alexander to adopt his cousin's year of birth (Alexander never changed the date, only the year) and father's name. If anyone checked, they would find a man who fitted this description and it must have helped him to feel that he was secure and unlikely to be found out.

Bigamy is incredibly easy to commit. Records aren't cross-referenced at all. Common names like John Smith or Simon Brown recur all the time all over Britain. You could be married in Liverpool one month and Bristol the next, and only the people involved would ever know. Bigamists are usually caught out these days by family members, or by the DHSS or Inland Revenue, or any other agency that keeps a record of dependants. Eighty years ago these records did not exist and bigamy was much more common than anyone realizes. It was the crime of the poor: deserted wives and husbands often 'remarried' without having been officially widowed or divorced. Divorce was almost impossible for anyone without money. The grounds were also strictly limited: Henrietta could have divorced Alexander for adultery or desertion, but there were no grounds on which he could have divorced her. For a woman, divorce carried a tremendous social stigma. Apparently, Henrietta had once contemplated agreeing to divorce her husband, but her family persuaded her not to do so.

By now, so many people knew what I was doing that it became impossible to keep it secret. The media were becoming very interested and I was afraid that the story would be reported inaccurately. When I had begun to trace Catherine's father, I had expected a boring story of infidelity – perhaps a married man who had strayed, only to go running back into the safe haven of domesticity when confronted by the consequences of his moral lapse. Or perhaps a young man in the grip of a first love affair who then bowed to family pressure when it came to making a commitment. I had never for a moment imagined the kind of sensational story I was unfolding. But when I thought about it, Catherine was such an extraordinary woman, she was unlikely to have had an ordinary father. Alexander seems to have been as theatrical as his daughter – who loved acting out parts and being on the public stage – and he was certainly as much of a story-teller, though his stories were more dangerous and certainly less lucrative. I remembered being told that Catherine's grandfather warned her as a child that her story-telling would get her 'into the clink or into the money' someday. It put Catherine in the money, but put her father on the wrong side of the law.

The speed at which things were accelerating pushed me into going public before I planned to do so, but it gave me the chance to choose which of the media outlets would be both responsible and deal with the story with integrity. Eventually, after discussions with the Pate family, I chose a BBC local television unit, who I knew would do a 'quality' job, and a national newspaper, edited by someone I trusted. The family donated the money paid for the photographs in the article to charity, in the best Catherine Cookson tradition. At this stage I worried very much about what I was doing to their lives – I knew that my research was going to change things for people, not always for the better – but things had progressed too far now to halt them.

I went to visit Reg and Betty Pate in Hertfordshire with a television crew in tow: they were friendly and welcoming, very happy to be interviewed on camera, and opened up their home, their memories and their family photograph albums for us. Reg talked quite a lot about his father Alexander. Photographs showed him to have been every bit as handsome as his errant father. He also had the same aristocratic look that had been commented on – the manner that had led Mary and Kate Fawcett to believe that the miner's son from Lesmahagow was a gentleman. On one of the photographs of Alexander on the grouse moors of Scotland in plus fours, with a gun on his shoulder, someone had scribbled across the bottom 'Lord McPate!'

Other photographs showed a very well-dressed, elegant man carrying a silver-topped cane. When I pointed to it, Reg told me that this cane had been given to his father by his father Alexander. Although Reg didn't know about the change of name, he told me that since Henrietta's funeral, the two Alexanders, father and son, had been in regular, though secret, contact. The women of the family would not have approved, he said. And that was how the cane had come to be transferred. Neither he nor Betty were Cookson fans and neither knew of the silver-topped cane that Catherine's father was noted for. It was another little piece of the jigsaw that fitted – another link between Alexander Pate and Alexander Davies.

Reg took me to visit his mother Elsie Moul, almost a hundred years old but still bright and lucid, although now

'Lord McPate' – Alexander jnr and his family.

living in sheltered accommodation. Elsie was initially a little confused by so many new people around her, but soon settled down and – with the cameras very much in the background – we were able to chat. She had kept the family secrets all her life, but there were some that she was now willing to talk about. I asked her what kind of person Henrietta had been. Elsie had not liked her mother-in-law and thought that there might be reasons why Alexander had left her. 'She had a hard life,' Elsie said, 'but she helped to make it. She was a hard woman.' She paused and then added, 'She was as hard as bricks. There was no love in her.' She repeated the last phrase two or three times – 'There was no love in her.'

Elsie Moul with her son Reg and the author.

The mysterious man with the silver-topped cane.

Had she known Alexander? I asked. At first she shook her head, but then told how she wasn't supposed to know who he was, or to see him, and that he had come to the back-door of their house several times asking for her husband. 'I knew it was him,' she said. She described the man whose appearance we were now familiar with and looked over all the family photographs we had brought, but Elsie was unable to confirm that Alexander appeared in any of them. Henrietta had apparently destroyed them all after he left. Only one was a possibility, a shot of a very young Elsie on the beach with an older man holding a silver-topped cane. Was it the younger or the older Alexander? They were both so alike. And who was the person holding the camera? Elsie couldn't remember.

To Reg's great regret, now that he knew its significance, the silver-topped cane that had been handed on from father to son had been lost when she moved out of her house into sheltered accommodation in July 2000. No one had any use for it now.

At the end of a very long day I felt tired, but utterly elated. I had finally, against all the odds, managed to talk to someone who had actually met the man I believed to have been Catherine Cookson's father.

12

MARGARET/ELIZABETH SMITH

There were still a lot of loose ends in the story. One of them concerned the family of Foster Smith – Alexander's nephew by marriage and the real father of his adopted daughter. I had traced quite a number of people in order to find him and had a considerable family tree for Jane Foster/ Williamson/Davies and her family, as well as a whole box of certificates. I wondered whether the family would be interested in having them. Again, tracing their addresses through electoral rolls, I wrote letters to surviving descendants of Foster Smith – the children and grandchildren of his daughter Olive. One of them replied. Olive's daughter Sally wrote that she and her sister Margaret would be delighted to find out more about their family tree. After exchanging lively emails with one of Sally's daughters, I arranged to go over to the north-east to meet them. Sally still lived in Backworth, just north of Newcastle, though the mines that had provided work for so many of her ancestors are no longer there. Today there are green fields behind the leafy streets instead of slag heaps.

Sally was welcoming and talkative, Margaret rather more shy. They were very pleased to see the pile of birth, marriage and death certificates that told the life stories of Jane and her family. They told me, as Kathy had, that although Foster's second daughter had been christened Jane she was always known in the family as Jenny in order to distinguish her from her great-aunt, Jane Davies.

Jane and Alexander had been known in the family as Ma and Pa Davies. Foster's oldest daughter Olive – seven years old when her sister Jenny was born – had lived with her father when he was lodging with the Davieses and had been old enough to remember Jane and Alexander well. Both she and Foster had talked about them often. Pa Davies was evidently a bit of a character – what was known in the north-east as a 'hook', another word for a crook. He'd been a story-teller, a smooth talker. Someone had once said that he was like the 1940s film star, John Laurie. They confirmed that he'd been a bookie, although much of the money he made had been gambled away again. Jane, his wife, had been pretty tough. She was the kind of woman, Sally said, who could make a Yorkshire pudding, a cake and a custard tart out of one egg and still have some over for breakfast! Jane had been trained to make every penny go a mile. She was also very strict. Everyone was adamant that if she had known about the bigamy, or Alexander's previous family, his life wouldn't have been worth living.

No one seemed very sure why contact between the two families had been broken after Jane and Alexander moved away from the area with Foster's younger daughter. Foster stayed in county Durham with his older daughter Olive, but

Sally Hall (left), daughter of Olive Foster Smith and Kathy Manning.

he did not keep in contact with Jenny. Did Foster Smith lose interest in the baby daughter he had seen for such a short time? Did he think it better that she have a new beginning with new parents? Or did the Davies become possessive about their adopted daughter and discourage contact? They certainly hadn't passed on much information. Olive had been brought up within the close-knit Foster family knowing almost everything about the family circumstances, but Jenny seemed to have known much less about her real family and had passed on hardly any of what she knew to her own daughter. Kathy had repeatedly asked about her family history as she grew up, but had always been told 'You don't want to

147

know. It was hard. Too hard.' As Jenny grew older she became more and more reclusive and was very bitter about her childhood. Like Catherine Cookson, Jenny was deeply traumatized at what she saw as her father's rejection of her. She suffered periods of severe depression and found it hard to form loving relationships. Whenever Kathy had tried to show her mother affection, Jenny would shrug her away saying, 'You're too soft. You have to be tough to survive.'

And what had happened to Margaret/Elizabeth? Sally and Margaret were able to tell me that it was indeed the same person, though known by two different names. She had been born Margaret Elizabeth Young, not Margaret Lizzie. I had been unable to find her correct birth certificate because she had been born in Ireland. She was most famous in the family for having been a medium, which explained Foster's interest in spiritualism. Apparently Foster was quite good at it and his party-trick had been to levitate a piano! This took some believing, but I was assured that it was true. Margaret had been an invalid from the beginning, and might have suffered from post-natal depression – barely recognized at the time as a 'proper' illness and very hard to treat. But Sally had also been told by her mother Olive that Margaret had had TB and that she had spent a great deal of time in a sanatorium near Wooler in Northumberland. I wondered how this fitted with the fact that Kathy had been told by Jenny that Margaret was mentally ill and had been in the mental asylum (as it was then known) in Morpeth before dying of cancer. Yet the two stories were not incompatible and both could well have been true. Big institutions were breeding grounds for contagious diseases such as TB; there was an epidemic during the 1920s, with almost a thousand people a week dying from it. Margaret could have caught TB while being treated for depression. But mental illness carried such an enormous social stigma, it was quite normal for families to 'cover up' its occurrence. I needed to find Margaret's death certificate in order to be sure.

The picture that was emerging was that after Olive's birth Foster's wife became ill, possibly with post-natal depression, possibly TB, and was hospitalized, leaving her baby to be looked after by Foster's aunt Jane with whom they were living. Margaret was in and out of hospital and eventually, in 1920, while living with her husband and daughter at 9 Victoria, again lodging with Alexander and Jane Davies, she gave birth to another child they called Jane, after her aunt. By a strange coincidence both Olive and Jane were born on the same day – 8 June – seven years apart. Once again Margaret became ill and she had to return to hospital. Olive was old enough for Foster to look after her, but he couldn't manage a baby as well, so little Jenny, as she was known by then, was left with her aunt and namesake, Jane Davies. Margaret Smith was never able to care for her children again. Sally showed me a photograph of her grandmother, taken in the 1920s. It is a very sad image of a sick woman sitting between two unidentified women – the one on the left is in the same uniform, though with the collar unbuttoned, and is probably a fellow patient. The other girl may well be a visiting relative. The uniforms made it more likely that Margaret was being cared for in the county mental hospital rather than a sanatorium. We rephotographed the faded and rather damaged snap and were able to make another print to send to Kathy in America. She had never seen a photo of her grandmother before.

149

Margaret Elizabeth Smith (centre).

I went to the record office in Morpeth to look for the death certificate, or funeral record, of Margaret Smith and was horrified to see how many people committed to the county mental hospital had actually died while resident there. Admittedly some of them were very old and senile (presumably for people with Alzheimer's, this was the only place to go) but large numbers were in their twenties, thirties and forties. No causes of death were noted on the church records that listed their funerals, so there was no way of knowing why so many died. I was beginning to understand my own grandmother's dread of having to be admitted to a place such as Morpeth: mental illness carried an enormous stigma in society at the beginning of the century and treatment was often barbaric. The fact that many mental hospitals had previously been workhouses must have added to the horror. Once inside, it was very difficult to get out again. The records made very depressing reading. But though I found two other members of Margaret's family who died in Morpeth, I didn't find Margaret herself, and needed to widen the search. Foster, I knew, had been living in Holywell Square, Backworth, by 1930 and I began to look for records in the Tynemouth and North Shields area of Tyne and Wear. Eventually I found what I was looking for.

Margaret Elizabeth's life had been tragic. Unable to look after her own children, unable to live with her husband except for short periods, she spent nearly twenty years in and out of hospital until she died in 1933 in a small nursing home in North Shields – not from tuberculosis, but from cancer of the womb. Tragic, too, for her husband, as there was no possibility of divorce from a spouse suffering from mental illness. Foster

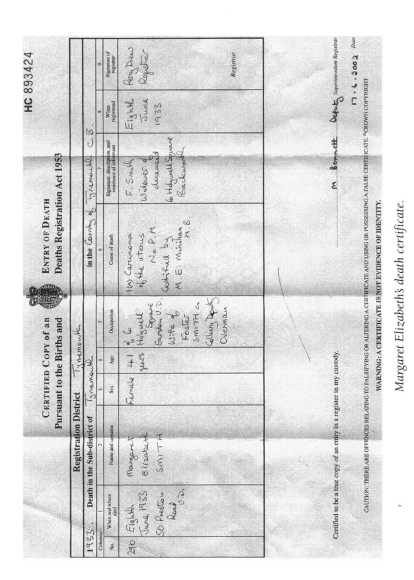

Margaret Elizabeth's death certificate.

lived for much of his married life alone, earning the money for his daughter's keep. When Olive was old enough she kept house for her father and when she married at eighteen she and her husband continued to live with him. Their first child, born in 1932, was named Margaret after her grandmother. Apparently Margaret senior was well enough on one occasion after baby Margaret's birth to come home and sit out in the garden with the baby in the pram. Margaret Elizabeth told Olive that she would never be well enough to see her grandchild grow up. The following year she died at the age of forty-one.

Eighteen months later Foster married Elspeth. This caused a few family ructions because she wouldn't agree to live with Foster's daughter Olive, who, even though she was eight months pregnant, had to move out. Elspeth was jealous of Foster's grandchildren, who never felt they could visit quite as freely as they would have liked. No one could remember his younger daughter Jenny ever being a visitor, though she had come up from Scarborough at least twice to see other relatives living in county Durham. No one seemed to know for sure whether she ever met her real mother. I wondered whether she had resented the way she'd been cast off by Foster and Margaret and passed on to Jane and Alexander like an unwanted Christmas parcel. Born on the same day, seven years apart, the girls' shared birthdays must have been annual reminders of their separation.

Sally and Margaret had been totally ignorant of Alexander's previous identity as Alexander Pate – just as the Pates had been unaware of their grandfather's metamorphosis into Alexander Davies. Sally and Margaret were very intrigued to find that the notorious Pa Davies might have been Catherine Cookson's father. True north-easterners, they were both admirers of her books and the television adaptations. Neither of them wanted any kind of publicity, but they were very happy to be put in touch with their cousin Kathy, with whom they had lost contact. They still talked of the day she had arrived at their mother Olive's front door as a young teenager, desperate to find her 'real' family.

We spent two or three hours talking and sharing stories and were so engrossed that it was not until we were walking down the path to the car that Sally and Margaret remembered that they had prepared a sumptuous tea with homemade scones and cakes and the best china. It was all laid out in the kitchen ready to bring in, but we had talked so much no one had even remembered to put the kettle on! Sally was mortified. It was too late to stay – I needed to make the long drive home in order to be back in time for another appointment, but I promised to make another visit – and this time would insist on tea! Privately I hoped that next time I would be able to bring their cousin Kathy. She was very keen to come over to England and re-establish contact with her lost relatives, and I had already tentatively floated the idea of a reunion – possibly even a get-together with the Pate family. It seemed important to have some kind of celebration that would bring the two halves of Alexander's life and his two families together.

13

---·•·---

FILMING

The BBC film, made in 2001, gave me the opportunity, for the first time, to tell the story from the beginning. Although the house where Catherine Cookson was brought up had been demolished, we found a narrow street in Tyne Dock almost identical to William Black Street. Each house was actually two tiny dwellings – an upstairs and a downstairs maisonette, though many of these houses have either been bulldozed down or converted into single dwellings. But in this street the front doors were still grouped together in pairs. Even the narrow alleys between the yards with their outside privies remained. It was in one of these alleyways that Catherine was told by her friends that she was illegitimate. A group of small children were playing in the street, kicking a tin can around, much as they did in Catherine's day. Apart from the fact that it all looked a bit more prosperous, nothing much had changed.

We went to the Ravensworth Arms, which was in the process of being gutted for refurbishment, revealing some of the original interior – the rooms where Kate had served behind the bar, the attics where she had slept. Standing at the attic window looking across to the site where Ravensworth Castle had once stood, I could imagine how Kate must have felt, knowing she was pregnant, waiting day after day for her lover to walk into the taproom, becoming increasingly desperate as the child inside her grew and quickened, until her condition could no longer be concealed.

From Lamesley we went to the windswept valley where Alexander Davies had lived at 9 Victoria Row with his bigamous wife Jane, and then to Scarborough, to Wykeham Street and the house where he had died. I kept wondering why Alexander had abandoned such a warm, sympathetic, fun-loving individual such as Kate in order to marry an older woman, who was by all reports a very tough character. Jane's character had been honed by hardship into something much less attractive. Perhaps he felt that Kate would not be so easy to deceive, and she certainly wouldn't have contemplated bigamy. That Alexander had wanted his freedom initially through divorce, and only committed bigamy as a last resort, we know from the Pate family. But this would not have been any use to Kate – as a practising Catholic, she couldn't have married a divorcé. For Alexander and Kate there would have been too many obstacles to a relationship. Three years later in Darlington – far enough south to make a new start, Alexander could approach Jane with a clean slate. The fact that she was well into her thirties and was unable to have children would be a favourable omen for Alexander. How he felt about the adoption of Jenny Smith eleven years later it isn't possible to know, but he seems to have mellowed as he grew older. I found it very poignant that he had abandoned four of his own children, only to bring up someone else's daughter.

Scarborough was a good choice for his retirement. It had a flourishing racecourse where he could continue his career as a bookie, and while it was close enough to the north-east to maintain whatever ties Alexander chose to keep, it was far enough away to make it less likely that he would bump into anyone who had known him in his previous life. It was also far enough from Foster Smith and his family to allow Jane and Alexander free rein with their adopted daughter without any interference from her relatives.

With Sheila and June I visited Alexander's unmarked grave in Scarborough cemetery. It was a cold wet day with a bitter east wind and the atmosphere was very sombre. For the first time, his Pate grandchildren were able to see where their grandfather was buried and lay flowers on his grave. It was an event that produced very mixed feelings: this was the man who had abandoned their mother Isabella before she was born, who had treated their grandmother Henrietta Waggott appallingly, a person who had cheated and lied. But he was still their grandfather. Sheila marked the grave with a temporary plaque to give the family time to think about a more permanent memorial. For me, knowing what I now knew about him, the bare, anonymous grass seemed somehow appropriate.

The main key to tracking Catherine's father had been her genetically transmitted disease – hereditary haemorrhagic telangiectasis. It is incredibly rare and can only be passed from parent to child. Alexander passed it to three out of his four known children and it proved to be the one fact that linked his two identities as well as his relationship to Catherine. Not only is the disease rare, there are two distinct types of it, and

157

both Alexander and Catherine had the same type – additional evidence of paternity. It is ironic that Catherine put so much money into research for the one condition that could link her incontrovertibly to her real father. She gave a great deal to charity, but one of her most generous acts was to fund research into genetically transmitted diseases – including her own – at Newcastle University medical school. Her grant funded the 'Cookson mouse', a genetically modified mouse that, it is hoped, will eventually provide not a cure but a solution for sufferers of HHT, by replacing the faulty genes within the cells with healthy ones. Newcastle now has one of the best genetic units in Europe, thanks to Catherine's generosity. One of the spin-offs has been the advance of DNA testing within the unit mainly for forensic purposes, but also to solve private cases of uncertain paternity. The very research that Catherine funded could now finally solve the problem of her father's identity beyond all doubt. DNA from his descendants could be matched against her own profile to prove the link.

When I was working on Catherine's biography, the one thing that had really puzzled me was why, when the identity of her father had been so important in her life, and when she had earlier gone to such lengths to find out who her father was, she never had him traced. For most people, tracing relatives is difficult and expensive, so they either do it themselves, or give up. But Catherine had the money to pay a professional genealogist to do it for her – but chose not to. In countless interviews with the press she would speculate on her absent father. She never denied outright that her father could have been a member of the aristocracy, or at least a gentleman in the old-fashioned sense, though she wrote in

Our Kate that, after conversations with her mother before she died, she always mentally put inverted commas around the word – the inference being that he wasn't a gentleman at all. Yet she always left the door open for public speculation, unable to destroy the comforting myth she had spent most of her young life creating. She preferred the father she had created for herself, rather than the character that Kate had described.

Her cousin Theresa, Aunt Mary's daughter, is one of the few members of Catherine's family willing to talk freely on the subject. Though much younger, Theresa had quite a lot of contact with Catherine as a child and often stayed at the Hurst. Her mother Mary was one of the few people who had known the real Alexander, or 'Alec' as they knew him. Theresa describes Catherine as having been a 'difficult' child who grew up into a wilful, highly strung, complicated young woman. She felt her illegitimacy deeply – as she felt everything deeply. Some of her cousins thought that she had been spoilt, first by her grandparents, who doted on her, and then by Kate, who suffered an enormous amount of guilt where her only daughter was concerned.

There was a large tribe of cousins around when Catherine was growing up – all younger than she was. Kate's sister Sarah married a miner called Mick Lavelle and Mary married Alec Charlton. Kate, who had had ambitions to find someone better, urged her sisters to marry – even the hard lot of a miner's wife, she said, was better than her own fate. As an adult, Catherine was closest to her cousin Sarah, the youngest child of her aunt Sarah. Cousin Sarah and her husband Jack were frequent visitors at the Hurst and when Catherine went north on writers' book events, it was Sarah she often stayed with. Mary's daughter Theresa was another favourite. She was only a child when Catherine first bought the Hurst and was sometimes invited to stay there and be a companion to Catherine's friend Nan Smyth's mentally handicapped daughter Maisie. Theresa has vivid memories of her visits there.

Theresa told me some of the stories that her mother Mary had passed on. Alec was a 'toff', tall and good-looking and very well spoken, though where the miner's son from Lesmahagow had learned his manners was a mystery. Perhaps, like his daughter Catherine, he had the ability to act a part, a desire to better himself. For years Catherine herself laid claim to a much better background than was really the case.

One thing still bothered me, and that was whether Kate had known about the bigamous marriage. I thought it was possible that she did. She was still so passionately attached to him that it would be incredible if she hadn't continued to try to make contact with him. After Catherine's birth Kate was working in Gateshead, which is a long way from Darlington, but it is possible that she heard about him from mutual acquaintances. One of the witnesses to Alexander's second marriage was William Fawcett, a member of the large Fawcett clan in the north-east and bearing the same name as Kate's father. I could find little about him other than that he too worked for the drapery firm of Richard Luck. William's father, who had died while he was a child, had been a marine engineer sailing out of Hartlepool. His elder brother was also a marine engineer. Maybe this was where Alexander had got his notion of passing himself off as a marine engineer. At no point in Alexander's life did I find any other mention of his sea-going days except on the death certificate signed by George Crosby. Alexander's adopted daughter Jenny always put him down as a 'labourer, retired', which seems closer to the truth. Alexander seems to have been a man for whom the truth mattered little.

14

A FAMILY REUNION

I had to wait more than a year to meet Alexander's step-grandaughter Kathy. A planned visit to England had to be postponed in the wake of the 11 September tragedy and Kathy wasn't able to come again until the following June. She went first to Scarborough – the first time she'd been there since her mother died – and it was a very emotional visit. Kathy had to relive some painful experiences, most of them relating to her mother. Jenny had passed on the pain of her own unloved childhood: what she had suffered at the hands of her foster mother Jane Davies, and the trauma of being abandoned by her real parents, had warped her character and rendered her incapable of being a loving mother to her own daughter. Kathy was afraid of her mother. Nothing she did was ever good enough for her and what little confidence Kathy had as a child was completely eroded by Jenny's destructive criticism. Kathy had also suffered from Jenny's neurotic inability to accept change. Although they could afford it, Jenny had refused to have a bathroom installed. Kathy had felt humiliated as a teenage girl by the fact that she was the only one at her school who didn't have a bathroom or inside toilet. She said it made her feel dirty.

Even after Kathy left home and established a successful career for herself, Jenny still had the power to reduce her to that nervous, insecure child again whenever they met. On a visit from the States Kathy had brought American filter coffee which Jenny wouldn't allow her to use, but forced her instead to drink the instant coffee she knew she hated. When Kathy made a move to help her sick father eat his breakfast, her hand had been slapped away with a bitter comment. Kathy told me that when her mother died and she flew back from America for the funeral, so powerful were her negative feelings towards the house, she had been unable to go inside when she first arrived. Even when she managed to conquer this feeling she still couldn't bring herself to spend the night in the house and had to stay in a bed and breakfast.

Three generations: Margaret Elizabeth, Jenny and Kathy.

Kathy (right), Alexander's step-grandaughter with the author.

Kathy came straight from Scarborough to visit me. Some people are very different to their telephone persona, but Kathy was the same shy, courteous but very warm person I had talked to and exchanged emails with. She dispelled my concern at the disruption to her life caused by my research saying that all this knowledge had helped her to understand her mother, and that she was grateful to me for bringing her together with the family she had never been given the opportunity to know.

Kathy had brought over many more documents she had unearthed among her mother's possessions. Among them were two wills made by Alexander Davies. One of them was

This is the Last Will and Testament

of me *Alexander Davies* of *5 Wykeham Street*

in the County of *Scarbrough Yorkshire*

I hereby revoke all wills and testamentary instruments heretofore by

me made. I appoint_____ of_____

and_____ of_____

to be the Executors of this my Will. I direct my Executors to pay

my just debts and Funeral and Testamentary Expenses.

I give and bequeath

two miss jane Smith All money House And furniture
And All Personal belongings

Witness my hand this_____ day of_____ 19___

(Testator to sign here)_____

If necessary to use next page, strike this out.

Signed by the above-named Testator as h___ last Will in the presence of us both, being present at the same time, who in h___ presence and in the presence of each other have hereunto subscribed our names as witnesses.

Witnesses to sign here with their address and occupation.

Harry Wilburn Patrick & Mary Jane Westwood, 7 Wykeham St
51 Gladstone Road Scarboro' Scarbro gh *House wife*
Laundroman S.B.R

Alexander's will.

166

dated 25 September 1933 and written in Hunwick. Under 'I hereby give and bequeath unto' Alexander had written in his own strong hand: 'Jane Davies my wife I leave Everything I posses[sic] to her'. It was signed by Sarah Barraclough and Joseph Fenwick. The other will had been written after the death of Jane Davies in 1945 and the handwriting was shaky and frail. In this version Alexander gave and bequeathed 'two [sic] miss jane smith All money House And furniture And All personal belongings'. It was signed by a friend, Harry Welburn Patrick and the next-door neighbour, Mary Jane Westwood.

There was another big surprise. Among the documents Kathy brought was a mortgage dated 29 November 1910 for a house bought by Jane Davies in Hirst near Ashington in Northumberland. This confirmed for me that Alexander had migrated north from Darlington after his marriage, and I could establish where he had spent the years of the First World War. Jane's sister Margaret (Foster Smith's mother) was currently living in Morpeth, and Jane's nephew Foster was working in the pits near Ashington. The house in Ariel Street seems to have been run by Jane as a lodging house, with her nephew as one of the lodgers. It was here in Ashington that Foster met his wife Margaret Elizabeth Young. The mortgage, for £250 8/s 6d, had been taken out with the Tynemouth Permanent Benefit Society – a bold, innovative move for the miner's widow. I wondered where she had found the deposit: perhaps by being very stringent financially, she had managed to save a small nest-egg; or perhaps Alexander had had a particularly big win on the horses. Again there was a sad irony that while his real wife Henrietta was living in poverty at the mercy of relatives, his bigamous wife should be buying a house twenty miles further north.

Kathy talked about the photographs that had been displayed on the sideboard and the mantelpiece during her childhood. One in particular showed Jane Davies sitting in a chair, a plain, buxom woman with big teeth; her one good feature, her beautiful hair, was piled in big curls on top of her head. Behind her stood the man that Kathy's mother had always referred to as 'me fathar', although she called him Uncle Alec face to face. Kathy said he looked a lot younger than his wife, and though he only admitted to a two-year age difference, his real birth certificate showed that there were actually six years between them. As they aged the gap visibly widened: while Alexander mellowed into a distinguished older man, Jane Davies had had a hard life and had not worn well.

The mortgage on Jane Davies' house.

I wondered how Alexander had managed to keep his double life so secret, but Kathy said that he had often been away for a week at a time on business connected with the horses. After one of these mysterious absences he would either come back broke to face Jane's fury, or with his pockets bulging with notes. Going away to the races, it would have been easy for Alexander to keep in contact with his son without his wife Jane knowing. Kathy's mother Jenny was a different matter. She looked after Alexander for three years after Jane died, and for the last year Kathy's father was there to help her. From little snippets of information they let slip from time to time, Kathy suspected that Alexander had talked more freely to them about his life. Her mother had also found – and kept – the birth certificate that revealed his true identity. Kathy speculated that that might have been the main reason why she had not erected a headstone for him, even though she lavished large sums on his coffin and the funeral. Kathy said that later on her mother had also begun to collect Catherine Cookson books, though she denied reading them. If she had read them, particularly *Our Kate*, Kathy thought that her mother must have been aware of the shared hereditary disease, and the details of the name on Catherine's birth certificate. It was quite possible that Kathy's secretive, reclusive mother could have put two and two together.

The mental health problems that had made Margaret Elizabeth Smith's life so tragic had also been passed on to her daughter Jenny, and this inherited tendency to depression was exacerbated by the circumstances of her childhood and her sense of abandonment by her real parents. In middle age the depression became more pronounced: on one occasion Kathy

The bill for Alexander's funeral.
Note the instruction for the 'best coffin'.

remembered her mother running out of the house because she couldn't bear the sound of the rain on the windows. Eventually Jenny had required treatment in the York mental hospital, though modern psychiatric care was mercifully more advanced than it had been in Margaret's day and she was quickly released. When Kathy was growing up it was her greatest fear that this mental instability might have been passed on to her in her genes, but it is obvious to anyone spending time in her company that her great strength of character owes much more to the inherited stoicism and courage of those amazing women who lived at Newfield, bringing up football teams of children in tiny rooms on hardly any money at all. Kathy and her partner both work for US social services finding placements for children who have been the victims of abuse and who are too damaged for ordinary foster homes.

One of Kathy's objectives in coming over to England was to visit her cousins Sally and Margaret in Backworth. Their mother Olive was dead, but they had all been told the story of Kathy's arrival on the doorstep, as a distressed fifteen-year-old, desperate to see her relatives and meet her 'real' grandfather, Foster. Kathy told me how she had left home not even knowing her aunt Olive's address, but using money in her post office account she had taken the bus from Scarborough to Newcastle and then another bus out to Backworth. When she got off at the stop, she had asked a man if he knew where her aunt Olive lived – a risky move seen from today's perspective, but in those days communities were smaller and more intimate and there was a greater degree of trust. The man told her to follow him and he took her straight to her aunt's door. Kathy announced to Olive: 'I'm Jenny's daughter and I've come to see my Grandad.' Olive's first words were 'Does your mother know you're here?'

Kathy replied that she had run away. 'Well, you can see your grandad today,' Olive retorted, 'but you're going straight back on the bus tomorrow!'

Olive took Kathy across the fields to Shiremoor where Foster was living. Kathy described how they had found him in bed, ill with the severe lung problems that dogged him in later life, a legacy of all the coal dust he had inhaled. When Kathy came into the room he sat up, and when Olive asked 'Do you know who this is?' he nodded and wheezed, 'That's our Jenny's bairn'. Kathy was touched that he recognized her so readily. It was the first and only time he had seen his granddaughter. The visit was cut short by the arrival of his second wife Elspeth, whose manner was far from welcoming, and they left.

Two years after this visit north Kathy left home for good, eventually settling in America in 1970. The tenuous contact with Olive and Foster was never kept up and after they died she didn't know where the rest of her north-eastern relatives were living. Kathy was understandably apprehensive at meeting Olive's daughter Sally, who by an amazing coincidence lived only a few doors away from the house where Kathy had once visited her aunt. But the welcome that she was given in Backworth quickly dispersed any doubts she might have had about whether the family would be pleased to see her again. Sally relayed all the stories that her mother Olive had told her about the reasons why her mother Jenny had been taken away by the Davieses and had had so little contact with her blood relations.

Jenny had been jealous of Olive, because Olive was being brought up by her real father and – when she was well enough – her mother. She used to tell Kathy that Olive was at home being spoilt rotten while she had to be 'a skivvy' for Ma Davies. Jenny rarely talked about Jane Davies and never with affection: all her affection was reserved for the man she called 'Uncle Alec' to his face, but 'me fathar' or 'the fathar' to everyone else. Her bitterness at being given away by her real father and mother destroyed her life. Olive, on the other hand, had always imagined that Jenny was 'a little princess', being given a privileged upbringing by the Davieses, who were rumoured in the family to have money. They owned their own house in Scarborough, while Foster Smith still lived in a colliery house. In reality Olive spent her childhood being a

Foster Smith's older daughter Olive and her husband Tommy.

173

skivvy for her father and the lodgers. Because of her mother's ill-health and being away in hospital for long periods, it fell on Olive to shoulder much of the housework.

Sally was able to tell us that when Olive was a young child, she and Foster had lived most of the time with Ma and Pa Davies, although Olive didn't like them much, especially Alexander. His favourite was Jenny and Olive said that he would lose no opportunity to pit one child against the other. When they were all still living at 9 Victoria in Witton le Wear, Olive was smacked because one evening when she was washing the three-year-old Jenny she playfully poured some cold water out of the kettle spout on to Jenny's neck. The little girl thought that it was boiling hot and screamed loudly. Alexander wouldn't listen to Olive's explanation and berated her thoroughly for making her sister cry. It was only one of many incidents that had contributed to Olive's dislike of 'Pa Davies'. The shared household came to an end abruptly when Jenny was about three and Olive ten. No one in the family seemed to know why, but afterwards there was a huge rift and close contact between them was broken, even though Foster was still living at Victoria and the Davieses three miles away at Willington and Hunwick. When Alexander and Jane Davies moved to Scarborough in 1933 Jenny didn't see her real father Foster again.

The following evening, accompanied by Sally and her daughter, I took Kathy, the adopted granddaughter of Alexander Davies to meet the granddaughters of Alexander Pate. It seemed incredible to me that, after so much time, the families of Foster Smith and that of his friend Alexander Davies Pate lived only three miles apart and had never known anything about each other.

The reunion: Kathy, Judith (Sally's daughter), Sally and Sheila.

June was unfortunately away, but Sheila was at home. Although Kathy was nervous about the meeting Sheila welcomed her as a member of the family. For the first time the two halves of Alexander's life came together in the same room. Over coffee and cakes, Sheila told stories of Alexander in his Pate identity, and Sally and Kathy told stories they had heard from their mothers about the man they knew as Alexander Davies. They also discussed the damage that had been handed on from generation to generation as a result of the havoc that he had caused in their parents' lives. Sheila and her siblings had been brought up very strictly and with a deep suspicion of men, particularly good-looking ones. They had been closely watched and never been allowed to gamble in any way – 'We weren't even allowed to play cards,' Sheila said. Kathy and Sally had had their lives blighted by the rift that had occurred between Alexander and Foster, that had caused their mothers to be separated as children.

We left Sheila's house a lot later than we had planned, but there was a definite sense of completion. Alexander was beginning to emerge as a real person, and between us we had managed to make some sense of his double life. There were things that would always cause grief – among them his abandonment of the Pate children and the fact that he left all his property to his adopted granddaughter when his own children were still struggling. What Alexander's feelings were to the family he left behind, we will never know. His sister Jeanie – the one person who would know – died in 1985, and never married.

And then there was Catherine Cookson, whose entire life had been shaped by Alexander's abandonment, but who had made millions 'writing it out'. If Alexander had been able to marry Kate, if Catherine had been born legitimate, would she have written a novel at all? Catherine herself was always very clear that much of her motivation was owed to her absent father. 'My bitterness . . . is not for myself because I realize now that in being part of "the gentleman" – and I have my tongue in my cheek even as I write the word – I have a great deal to be thankful for, for he provided the norm at which I aimed. It was him in me that pushed and pulled me out of the drabness of my early existence. It was from him that I got the power to convey awareness, this painful sensitivity, without which what I sensed in others would have remained an untranscribable mass of feelings. Yet should I be thankful?

Wouldn't it have been much easier for me if, having been born sixteen years later, I had inherited David McDermott's utter placidity? With this trait, and a touch of my mother's sense of humour, life would have been a straight line track, no sharp bends, no uphill pulls . . . no summit."* And probably no novels either – that much is implicit in the text.

*From the Catherine Cookson Collection in the Howard Gotlieb Archival Research Centre at Boston University.

15

HOW MUCH DID CATHERINE KNOW?

I became increasingly convinced, while researching Catherine's story, that she knew much more than she had ever allowed anyone to suspect about her father and his relationship with Kate. But only once during her life, in an interview with BBC Northeast and Cumbria, did Catherine admit that she knew who her father was, though she said that she was never going to reveal his identity. She stated emphatically that the knowledge would go to the grave with her and with Kate. This was the only time Catherine ever admitted that her mother had told her about Alexander, during the time Kate had spent with her in Hastings just before she died.

After Kate's death, Catherine sat down in the room where she had nursed her mother, on the ground-floor of the house next to the kitchen, and began to write her autobiography. It was an act of catharsis, an attempt to 'write out' the anger and bitterness she felt about the circumstances of her childhood, and in particular her father's absence. The first versions of the book were called 'From the Seed of all Sorrow' and large sections of the text were edited out or rewritten when it was published twelve years later as *Our Kate*. The early manuscripts are in the archives of Boston University, USA, and they make interesting reading. Some of the passages that did not appear in *Our Kate* concern her feelings towards her father, the 'gentleman' she had spent so many years fantasizing about, and they make it clear that she knew a great deal about his real character. He was a 'scoundrel' and a weakling, someone who ran away from domestic dramas and emotional demands. Someone who pretended to be a gentleman, but was not.

'Gentleman! He was a skunk, wasn't he? But did I blame him? No, not one iota . . . only when the years of longing to see his face, to hear his voice had turned sour on me; only when the seed he had set and left to grow up in an environment of fear and shame, of drink and poverty, took its toll in later years, only then did I see him as a weakling . . . a weakling with which I am stuck, for I am he in part as much as I am Kate. Can we [ever] claim to be ourselves?'*

Among the more valuable parts of his legacy, for Catherine, was his theatricality – Catherine loved being on the public stage. Even as a small child she would roll back the hearthrug and perform singing and dancing routines for her grandparents; as an adult she would hold large audiences spellbound with her tales of life in William Black Street and the Harton Workhouse laundry. She had what was called in the north-east 'the gift of the gab'. Then there was Alexander's charm and good looks. Catherine certainly inherited those and was secretly very proud of the fact that people of both

*From the Catherine Cookson Collection in the Howard Gotlieb Archival Research Centre at Boston University.

sexes fell in love with her all her life. She inspired absolute devotion from those around her. It was perhaps easier for a woman to handle this kind of attention than a susceptible young man. Alexander did not cope with it well and became a victim of his sensual nature and his phenomenal attraction to women. Catherine understood some of this. In the novel she wrote after Kate died, called *The Gambling Man*, Rory, the gambler and eventual bigamist, is – like her father – fatally attractive to women. 'He had no false modesty about his personal attraction. He knew that many a back door would have been left open for him if he had just raised an eyebrow or answered a gleam in a hungry woman's eyes. He didn't class himself as particularly handsome but was aware that he had something which was of greater appeal. If he had been asked to define it he would have found it impossible; he only knew that women were aware of him. And he had liked the knowledge, it gave him what he called a lift.'[†]

Alexander's main legacy to his daughter was hereditary haemorrhagic telangiectasis, the disease that blighted the second half of her life with repeated haemorrhages. Towards the end Catherine was having two or three pints of blood transfused almost every month to keep her going. But here too Catherine also triumphed, using her great wealth to fund research into a solution for sufferers of the same disease. For those who inherit the gene in future the outlook is much more optimistic. Doctors hope that it will eventually be as simple as using a nasal spray to deliver modified genes to the faulty cells that cause the bleeding.

[†]From the Catherine Cookson Collection in the Howard Gotlieb Archival Research Centre at Boston University.

People often ask me how I feel about having traced Catherine's father. Though it's very satisfying to have been able to do it, I have mixed feelings. Certainly knowing who her father was has helped my understanding of Catherine's character and the internal forces that drove her, but uncovering such a tragic story of betrayal and abandonment has given me no pleasure at all. The only good thing that has come out of it has been the restoration of their 'lost' grandfather to the Pate family – who had wondered all their lives what had become of him.

Another positive result is for Jenny's daughter Kathy – I have been able to give her back her family and provide some understanding of the emotional politics that separated them all in the first place. Kathy and her cousins are planning a reunion in Florida later in the year – when they can spend time getting to know each other again. But for the Pates it's a mixed blessing: their grandfather's story is full of pain.

Tracing your ancestors can be extremely risky: you may discover an illustrious forebear (the aristocrats of Catherine's fantasy) or a convicted criminal. While searching for Alexander I decided to look up some of my own ancestors and discovered that my Irish great grandmother, whom I had thought a respectable farmer's wife, had lived above a tavern and given birth to three, possibly four, illegitimate children!

Rarely has a writer's childhood been as vital as Catherine's was to her. Friends have remarked that she could never have a conversation without referring to it in some way or other, and her father's absence – his nebulous identity – was crucial to her sense of herself. But while this generated tremendous insecurity in Catherine, it also created a gap that she could fill with her imagination. Alexander Davies died the year that Catherine finished *Kate Hannigan*: he would never know that his elegant legend had launched dozens of feckless male characters in the pages of her books, and that his daughter would make him famous as the man who had rejected her.

That Catherine knew both his identity and at least some of his history I have not the slightest doubt. When I reread the *The Gambling Man* during my search, not only was the plot too full of coincidences not to be significant – the hero's Scottish name, his smart appearance, his weak character, his preoccupation with gambling, his bigamy – there was also a very unusual surname. Catherine was very particular about names in her novels and often used and reused the names of people in the streets where she had grown up. By her own admission, real people – including members of her family – were the templates for her characters. In *The Gambling Man*, the name of Rory's first wife is Waggett – spelt with an 'e' instead of an 'o' – but still the same as Alexander's first wife Henrietta. It is not a common name in the north-east and there certainly weren't any Waggotts in Tyne Dock. It was one coincidence too many. That's when I became certain that Catherine had known.

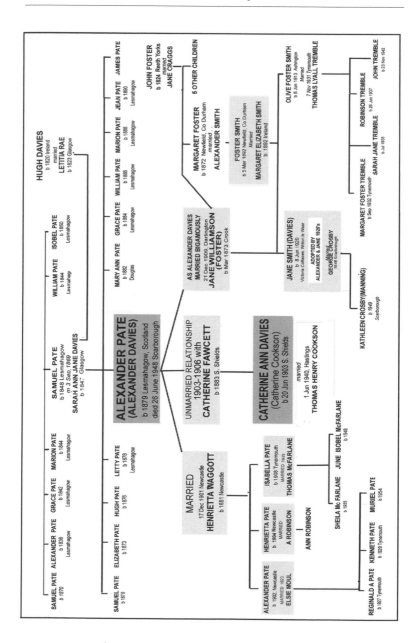

POSTSCRIPT

———•·•———

FINDING YOUR
OWN ANCESTORS

Delving into your own family history can be great fun and, although time-consuming, is very easy to do. The St Catherine's Index is usually the starting point for anyone tracing their wider family. It contains a record of every birth, marriage and death in England and Wales since civil registration was made compulsory in 1837. An index of Scottish records is available on the internet, or at the General Register Office in Edinburgh and the Family History Centre in London. Irish records are held at the General Register Offices in Dublin and Belfast.

The St Catherine's Index for England and Wales is kept on microfiche and copies are held in all the County Record Offices around the country and at most main libraries. Finding a reference in the Indexes enables you to order copies of birth, marriage and death certificates for members of your family. Marriage certificates are useful because they give addresses for the bridegroom and the bride, their ages, occupations and the names and occupations of their fathers.

185

Recent death certificates give date and place of birth, name and address of next of kin and the deceased's usual address as well as the cause of death. Older death certificates give only the deceased's age at the time of death. Birth certificates give the names of both parents and their addresses and the father's occupation.

If you want to trace your own ancestors, start with information that you know to be true, as far back in time as you can safely go. Ask other family members for everything they can remember about their relatives, or any stories they've been told that might give clues to relationships, occupations, places your ancestors lived and any major events. The male line in the family is usually the easiest to trace initially, since women change their names on marriage. In order to find an ancestor you need to know their name and the place where they lived. The latter is very important if the name is a common one. A William Vipond will be very easy to find in the Index as it is unlikely that there are many of them, even if you don't know where the family lived. But a William Smith is a very different matter and you would need a much more accurate date and a specific place to narrow the search.

If you have your parents' marriage certificate, their age, occupation and place of residence will be on it as well as their fathers' names and addresses. This is a good place to start. It would also be useful to have your parents' birth certificates, since these will give you their mother's maiden names as well. Armed with these you will be in a position to find your grandparents. If you know how old your parents are and the ages of their brothers and sisters, you should be able to get an approximate date for your grandparents' marriage.

Once you have pinpointed a likely year, the next step is to find the certificate. The easiest way to do this is to go along to the nearest library that has a copy of the St Catherine's Index. At busy periods, i.e. evenings and weekends, you may have to book a microfiche reader. If you haven't used one before the library staff will be more than happy to show you.

Registration records for each year are broken down into quarters ending with the months March, June, September and December. Names are recorded in strict alphabetical order. If you know the year of marriage for certain, look through the four quarters of that year, bearing in mind the possibility of error. If you don't know an exact year, begin with the age of the oldest child and, starting with the year of their birth (never assume that a child was conceived in wedlock!), work backwards until you find a name that matches your grandparent. You may have to go back several years – people don't always have children straight away, or there may have been older children who died. If your grandfather's name was John Roberts and he married someone called Mary Grey and you know that they were living in Brighton when your father was born, you might look particularly for a Roberts married in Brighton. But bear in mind that marriages are usually held in the bride's parents' place of residence. When you find a John Roberts you think is likely, then look in the same quarter for a marriage registered under his wife's maiden name. If you find a Mary Grey married in the same quarter and the St Catherine's Index reference number is exactly the same for each entry, then you know you have found the right couple. The marriage certificate will give you your grandparents' ages and the names of their fathers so that you can go back yet another generation by looking for your grandparents' birth certificates.

The quarters are a record of the registration of an event, so someone born in November may not have been registered until January of the next year – always look through a whole quarter on either side of the critical year. Also bear in mind that people lie about their ages and be prepared to look through a few years on either side. For most twentieth-century births the mother's maiden name is in the Index as well as the father's name, the baby's Christian name and place of birth. This is invaluable for someone with a common surname such as Smith or Johnson. But for older births the mother's maiden name isn't listed in the Index.

If your grandfather's name was John Roberts and you know that he came from Birmingham, then note down each John Roberts born in that area during the critical year or years. Write down the quarter of each birth and the St Catherine's Index number on the microfiche. If there is only one possible individual then you can write to the General Register Office on Merseyside (address at the end of this chapter), enclosing a cheque for £8 and quoting the reference number and the other relevant details.

If there is more than one possible individual, then you can apply to the Register Office which covers the area of your grandfather's birth, e.g. Birmingham. Most libraries have a copy of the *Genealogical Services Directory* which lists all the Register Offices in the country. Write to the Superintendent Registrar, giving them your ancestor's name, age, father's Christian name, mother's maiden name if possible, exact date of birth if known, or the year and quarter of the birth as entered on the St Catherine's Index. Give the place of birth if known – a street, village, or town will do. If there are several individuals in the Index, list all the possible entries by quarter. Enclose a cheque for £7 and a stamped, self-addressed envelope. From the information you have given, the Registrar should be able to tell which one of the entries matches the details you are looking for and will send you the right certificate.

Additional information about the family can be obtained by going to the family history section of the library, or the relevant County Record Office. There you can look up the electoral rolls for the addresses on the certificates and find out who was living there. Before the franchise was extended to tenants as well as property-owners in 1918, you will have to rely on the Censuses. These start in 1841 and have been kept at roughly ten-year intervals until the present day – although recent Censuses aren't available until a hundred years has elapsed. Most libraries have pre-1901 Censuses for their own local area. A telephone call will establish which records they keep. The 1901 Census is available for the whole country over the internet on the Public Record Office site (see useful addresses at the end of the chapter) and the 1881 Census is also available for the whole country at your local library on CD-Rom. From the Censuses, you can find out who was living in the same household as your ancestors, the names and ages of other children, occupations of members of the family and where they were all born. It can also tell you the names of their neighbours and this can yield surprising information.

My great-grandfather's next-door neighbours had the same unusual surname as his mother and I discovered that they were his cousins and that the houses had once belonged to his maternal grandfather. A small girl further down the street had the same name and siblings as my grandmother and this explained how she had met her future husband. It would have taken me months of work to unearth all this information without the Census.

Parish records are held by the Record Offices for each county and you will probably have to make a telephone booking to see them. If your ancestors were married, baptized or buried according to religious rites, Catholic, Anglican or Free Church, the records should be there. All the information given on the registers is on microfilm and you can often find entire family records without having to send off for a single certificate. If the family was not religious – and a surprising number opted for civil marriages and never bothered to have their children christened – you will have to go back to the St Catherine's Index.

Before public registration became compulsory in 1837, the only records of marriage, birth and death are those of the parish in which the event took place. Pre-1837 research becomes more time-consuming and difficult, but is also very rewarding.

A great deal of information is now available on the internet, particularly at the Genuki site, where people all over the world have pooled their knowledge, making it available to everyone. Family history societies have also uploaded their research onto the internet. It is still patchy, but some parish records are also available, including those for the county of Durham, which have been painstakingly digitalized and are available on the internet covering nearly three hundred years (other counties have not even started). All the Scottish records up to 1900 – births, marriages, deaths, Census returns – are searchable on the internet, but not the English or the Irish. If you've never used the internet before, your local library will be very happy to let you use their computer for a small fee (as little as 50p per half-hour in some areas) and will show you how to use it.

Graveyards are wonderful sources of family history, though poorer families often couldn't afford headstones. County Record Offices and local libraries will also have maps and old photographs. The local papers are usually kept on microfilm at main libraries and they also yield obituaries, entries of marriage, birth and death – sometimes even wedding photographs. Trade directories may also be helpful if your ancestors practised a trade or were in business, and these go back quite a long way.

Beware of similar names when looking through the indexes. A typical selection of variations comes with Davies/Davis/ Davison; Smith/Smyth: Slight/Sleight; Foster/Forster; Cooper/ Cowper; Grey/Gray; Hewitson/Hewison; Johnston/Johnson; Thompson/Thomson; Waggott/Waggett – the list is almost endless. The further back in time you go, the more the names may differ. Members of the Pate family were often recorded as Peat in the seventeenth and eighteenth centuries. I also found one family listed as Portis, Portes, Portriss and Portresse. This can happen even for one individual – William Shakespeare spelt his own name in three or four different ways during his lifetime!

Some public records are only available from the Public Record Office at Kew. In particular they keep records of enlistment and discharge for the armed forces. If members of your family have been in the army, navy or air force then regimental museums and service organizations will often be able to give you information.

Not all family history is a straightforward account of births and marriages. If any member of your family has been adopted then the Family Records Centre near the Angel Islington in London holds indexes of legal adoptions since 1927. For divorces, the Central Register of Decrees Absolute holds records since 1858 and will do a ten-year search for a £20 fee.

Wills are an excellent source of information – not just property, but names and addresses of other family members. There are a number of Local Probate Sub-registries (addresses listed in the *Genealogical Services Directory*), but postal searches and copies can be obtained from the Probate Registry in York, or the Principal Probate Registry in London.

Finally, it can be great fun to join a local family history society. Some of these are specific to places, others for particular family names. Local libraries will be able to give you information on this, others are listed on the Genuki internet site and there is also a list in the *Genealogical Services Directory*.

USEFUL RESOURCES

St Catherine's Index – contains records of everyone's birth, marriage or death since registration became compulsory in 1837. Available in all central libraries and record offices on microfiche. Also now available at *www.1837online.com.*

1881 Census – a national record of where everyone was living in 1881, with details of their ages, places of birth, occupations, as well as those of their neighbours. Available at all central libraries and for purchase on CD-Rom from LDS Church Distribution Centre, 399 Garretts Green Lane, Birmingham B33 0UH at a price of £29.75, payable to 'Church of Jesus Christ of Latter-day Saints'.

1891 Census – as above, but only available on microfiche for a specific local area. You will have to go to a Central Library or Record Office local to the address you are searching.

1901 Census – available at local libraries as above. Can also be accessed on the internet at the website of the Public Record Office.

Pre-1881 Censuses – ten year intervals, dating back to 1841 at local County Record Offices.

Parish records – for baptisms, religious marriage ceremonies, and funerals. These can be found in the relevant County Record Offices.

School records – these are usually kept in the County Record Office.

Electoral rolls – for most of the twentieth century these can be seen in the County Record Office local to the address you are searching for. Current ones are held by the libraries.

Scottish records at *www.scotsorigins.com* or at Edinburgh General Register Office, New Register House, Edinburgh EH1 3YT. *www.gro-scotland.gov.uk*.

Irish records at the Dublin General Register Office for all Irish records pre-1922. Joyce House, 8–11 Lombard St East, Dublin 2, or the National Archives, Bishop Street, Dublin 8. Post-1922 for Northern Ireland, see the General Register Office, Oxford House, 49–55 Chichester St, Belfast, BT1 4HL, or the Public Record Office, 66 Balmoral Avenue, Belfast, BT9 6NY Some are on the internet – see links on *www.genuki.org.uk*.

Public Record Office at Ruskin Avenue, Kew, Richmond, Surrey, TW9 4DU. Tel. 020 8876 3444 or *www.pro.gov.uk*.

Divorce decrees at Principal Registry of the Family Division, First Avenue House, 42–49 High Holborn, London WC1V 6NP. Tel. 020 7947 7000.

Wills at Principal Probate Registry, First Avenue House, 42–49 High Holborn, London WC1V 6NP. Tel. 020 7947 7000 or Postal Searches and Copies Dept., the Probate Registry, Duncombe Place, York, YO1 7EA. Tel. 01904 666777.

Family Records Centre holds the original indexes of birth, marriage and death in England and Wales since 1837, as well as indexes of Adoptions since 1927, plus a great deal of other relevant information. 1 Myddleton Street, London EC1R 1UW. Tel. 020 8392 5300.

General Register Office – copies of certificates can be obtained by post, quoting the correct St Catherine's Index number, from the GRO, Smedley Hydro, Southport, Merseyside, PR8 2HH.

192.com – subscribers can trace modern names, addresses and telephone numbers.

War Graves Commission – a record of those who died in battle during the last 100 years, at *www.cwgc.org* or Records & Enquiries section, CWGC, 2 Marlow road, Maidenhead, Berks SL6 7DX.

Merchant Marine Records at Public Record Office, Kew, and the Maritime Museum, Greenwich.

Armed Forces at Public Record Office, Kew.

Genealogical websites at *www.genuki.org.uk* The very best of the websites for the United Kingdom, with excellent links to others all over the world.

Genealogical Services Directory – useful handbook of sources, addresses and telephone numbers with relevant articles on how to use the information, published by GR Specialist Information Services, 33 Nursery Road, York YO26 6NN; price £4.95.

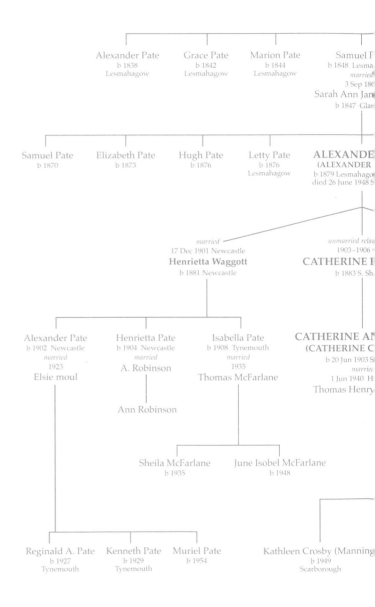

Alexander Pate
b 1838
Lesmahagow

Grace Pate
b 1842
Lesmahagow

Marion Pate
b 1844
Lesmahagow

Samuel F
b 1848 Lesma
married
3 Sep 186
Sarah Ann Jan
b 1847 Glas

Samuel Pate
b 1870

Elizabeth Pate
b 1873

Hugh Pate
b 1876

Letty Pate
b 1876
Lesmahagow

**ALEXANDE
(ALEXANDER**
b 1879 Lesmahago
died 26 June 1948 S

married
17 Dec 1901 Newcastle
Henrietta Waggott
b 1881 Newcastle

unmarried rela
1903–1906
CATHERINE I
b 1883 S. Sh

Alexander Pate
b 1902 Newcastle
married
1923
Elsie moul

Henrietta Pate
b 1904 Newcastle
married
A. Robinson

Isabella Pate
b 1908 Tynemouth
married
1935
Thomas McFarlane

**CATHERINE AI
(CATHERINE C**
b 20 Jun 1903 S
married
1 Jun 1940 H
Thomas Henry

Ann Robinson

Sheila McFarlane
b 1935

June Isobel McFarlane
b 1948

Reginald A. Pate
b 1927
Tynemouth

Kenneth Pate
b 1929
Tynemouth

Muriel Pate
b 1954

Kathleen Crosby (Manning
b 1949
Scarborough